The Redwing Blackbird's Song

The Redwing Blackbird's Song

Susan Phillips Speece

iUniverse, Inc.

New York Lincoln Shanghai

The Redwing Blackbird's Song

iUniverse books may be ordered through booksellers or by contacting:

iUniverse
2021 Pine Lake Road, Suite 100
Lincoln, NE 68512
www.iuniverse.com
1-800-Authors (1-800-288-4677)

ISBN: 0-595-34526-3 (pbk)
ISBN: 0-595-67125-X (cloth)

Printed in the United States of America

Contents

Acknowledgements

This book is dedicated to several people, my mother who always had faith in me and my two children, Ryan and Nicole who have always loved me even when I was not a perfect mom.

Introduction

As a child of the 50's and 60's growing up in the Midwest, there were certain expectations of young women. None of those expectations included having been a Dean of Mathematics, Science & Engineering or becoming the CEO of a successful regional college of a large land-grant university. Yet, I am happy to say that that is exactly where I find myself today. Over the years I have had many friends and acquaintances say that I should write my story. I always found that statement flattering but impractical, that was until recently. As I have progressed through the ranks of academe, I realize that I truly have been blessed and I have been successful in what I have done. Some would say that I have lead an extraordinary life. Often I am asked to give a motivational speech to groups of young women who have an interest in science, engineering, technology or mathematics. Sadly there still is a tendency in our society to discourage young women from choosing the scientific and technical fields. While the environment for young women is infinitely better than when I was growing up, we do have a ways to go before we reach parity. The stereotype still exists that assumes if you are a woman in the sciences you have to be tough as nails and any demonstration of being a woman is unacceptable. Well, as usual, I do not fit the stereotype. My entire life I have had a passion for the sciences and for people, more specifically for making a difference in the lives of others. I chose the field of teaching because I knew I could make a difference and I chose to write this book because I felt I might be able to make a difference in the lives of both men and women. I have faced obstacles and I have also been able to have a relatively normal life.

This book is not intended to only inspire women, I believe that the challenges that I have faced in my life are not unlike what many men and women face in their lives. Many of my challenges were prejudices against women in science, but there are many forms of prejudice that one faces in life and I hope that my life can encourage and inspire men and women alike. It is the spirit of the person, not their gender, color or other genetic characteristics that defines what they can and cannot do.

It was not until I met two men that I finally was motivated to tell my story. Dr. William Turner is a modern day Samuel Clements who not only is an internationally acclaimed wildlife sculptor, but also writes wonderful, charming memoirs of his life growing up in Eastern Virginia. I had the opportunity to read and edit a recent manuscript of Bill's and I suppose that inspired me to tell my story.

The other gentleman who encouraged me before, during and after the whole process of writing was my dear friend, Thomas M. Smith, Jr. Tom is an extremely successful businessman and president of a company that has repeatedly been named number one in the nation in its field. Tom and I have, from the first day we met, been able to tell each other anything and everything. There is a trust and comfort level in our friendship that makes that level of communication possible. Over a period of time I shared much of what is in this book with Tom. On many occasions he encouraged me to put it in print. He is my best friend and was the first one to have a chance to read some of the early edits, and he was the one I told, when I finally submitted the manuscript for publication.

When I speak to groups of young folks and try to encourage them to strive for excellence in their lives, I encourage them to find a mentor who can be their "cheerleader" and guide along their journey to what they will become. Perhaps this little book might become that mentor to those still striving for excellence in their lives.

Throughout this book I offer the reader an intimate glimpse into my life; the adventures of a little girl who would become a scientists, the struggles of a young woman to balance family and career and the abject fear one faces when one is stalked for far too many years. Several times after moving to Pennsylvania, I have often heard "you don't act like a college president." I take those comments as high compliments. What these folks are saying is that I am not stuffy and officious, rather I am down-to-earth and know how to laugh. I also break the stereotypic mold of a scientist. While I can carry on an intellectual conversation with science peers, I do not have to showcase my science knowledge when dealing with the general public, I can just be Susan.

As a child exploring the woods during summer vacations in upper Wisconsin I learned a fascination of nature and all of her glorious facets. I hope that I never lose that wonder and delight in nature and I hope I never lose the deep passion for making a difference in the lives of others.

1

Camp Conover

Ten weeks of nonstop meetings, travel and planning, ten weeks of 80 plus hours of work had left me drained and in serious need of recharging my batteries. Through the generosity of a friend I was able to get away to a cabin in the woods in eastern Virginia. Redwing blackbirds, laughing gulls, gold finches, cardinals and more, created an age-old song that lulled me in this idyllic setting in this isolated eastern Virginia wilderness. As I took in the sights, sounds and smells, I was transported back in time more than half a century to another place in time, a world away.

When I was a little child, my family used to go to Conover, WI for our summer vacations. My parents were able to rent a cottage for a few weeks and we were transformed from a suburban family to a family that could survive in the wilderness, or that's the way it seemed to a child of 6. Some mornings my father would get my brother and me up very early and we would go fishing for our breakfast. In our civilized world, no one would think of eating fish for breakfast, but in our little cabin in the Wisconsin woods, it was the very best thing one could have for breakfast. Freshly caught perch were the best, though sunfish were pretty darn good too. My mother would cook the fish up in a heavy iron skillet along with some eggs, ah; I can still remember the taste.

Some days Bambi would come to visit our little cabin. Truman, my brother, and I had named the semi-domesticated deer after the fabled Disney character. Bambi would cautiously approach the back porch looking for some scrap of food we might leave for it. Gingerly placing one hoof in front of the other she/he would advance on the smells emanating from the pan on the porch. We knew we had to watch from inside the house, because if we were outside, the deer would never get close. We knew it would be a great day if we got to see Bambi.

Besides the smell and taste of the freshly cooked perch, I most remember the sounds of the north woods. The crow was always the most vocal of our fellow vacationers, as I thought of them. Since we did not have crows in the Chicago suburbs, the caw of the crow would come to be associated with that summer cabin in the woods. Even today there is a little thrill of pleasure that courses through me when I hear the caw of the crows. Of course I now know the true nature of crows, but I am still pleased that I now live in an area where I hear the crows along with a host of other songbirds. Other voices I would hear on our little vacations would be that of the loon and the owls. But it has always been the happy 'okalee' of the redwing blackbird that has filled me with the joy, hope and the promise of spring.

I did not often hear the owls because I was usually asleep by the time they began their evening communications. It amazed me at how tired I became when the sun went down during those summer vacations. We would rise with or before the sun and retire with its setting, though there was always time to catch a few fire flies before going to bed.

It is odd, because I can recall playing in the woods around the cabin, I can remember the little oared fishing boat and I can still see my mother cooking the fish on a small stove at the end of a very narrow, very tiny kitchen, but I have no idea what my mother did to occupy her time during the days. I think Dad went out fishing later in the day without my brother and me (only so much sitting still a six year old and a 9 year old can do!) I know Truman and I played in the water at the edge of the lake, but mother was never a swimmer so she would not go into the lake. She may have watched us from the dock, but I just do not recall how she occupied her time.

I am not one of those persons who can remember exact conversations and interactions that took place when I was a child, I can recall some events and I greatly envy those who can recall details. My friend and writing inspiration, Dr. William Turner, an extraordinary sculptor and wonderful storyteller can recount, in detail, experiences he had as a child. As for me, I remember general experiences—flashes of images, brief conversations, but mostly I remember smells and sounds. I am sure some psychologist could take the above comments apart and offer a total psychoanalysis of me. I just think that some people's brains are able to track life's minutia while others track life's major twists and turns, just as some people are mathematically inclined and some are not. Try as I might, the one thing I cannot recall is ever seeing any interaction between my mother and my father that might constitute affection. I can recall one argument, but not the gentle play that goes on between a man and a woman in love. The only indication that I have that my father loved my mother comes from his behavior after she died—when he met someone from his childhood and married her a year later, he could not understand why they did not have the same kind of relationship the he and Mother had shared. He forgot that the relationship took 35 years to develop.

Lest you think my parents were unfeeling, I should say that my mother was always very loving toward my brother and me. I knew she loved me because she told me and she showed me. Patricia Carrie Harrity Phillips was a wonderful, gentle, caring woman, beloved in the family and in the community. Abandoned by her mother, she was raised by her maternal grandparents. She rarely spoke of her youth, but only indicated that her grandparents forced her to quit school when she was 13 so she could go to work and raise money for them. I have the impression that her life was very Spartan until she moved away from her grandparents and moved to Chicago. How I wish she were still around so I could ask her more about her youth and how she managed to migrate from Allentown, PA to Chicago. Sadly she died when she was only 57 and I was 22—we never had the chance to have those important adult-to-adult conversations. So many questions abound, but there are no relatives still alive to answer them. Life has come full circle since I was raised in the Chicago area and now live near Allentown, PA.

Mother was very bright and had she been around today, she would have been able to do anything she wanted. It was a given, if you needed someone to look over a paper you had written, Mom was the one to go to! She encouraged my brother and me equally and believed that we could do anything we set our minds to, though I suspected that she expected me to get married and just raise a family.

Dad was something else altogether. If you talk with any of my cousins, Uncle Trudy (my dad) was one of their favorite uncles. He was always positive and encouraging to them and to my brother, but to me, he was not accessible. He never encouraged me, never complimented me and never told me that he loved me. He would lavish praise on my brother (which was deserved), but for me there were only the leftovers. While this hurt as I was growing up and even when I began my profession, in many respects, I have him to thank for my success professionally. I never stopped trying to garner his praise and so have been driven to succeed.

One time I shared my sense of detachment with my father, with one of my cousins. He was totally surprised because he always knew my father to be loving and open to all of the cousins. He even mentioned that my dad would occasionally talk about my accomplishments (those times when my doing well would make him look good.) I am probably being overly critical of my father, he never beat me and he never denied me any of my needs. I suspect that he was proud of me, since he did talk about me to his friends, but he was raised in a time when women were possessions and their major functions were to raise children and keep a house. Letting a woman know that she was valued or loved was just not the manly thing to do.

Back to the summer time in Conover; another memory I have of our time in Conover is of an open commons area that must have been a part of the campgrounds. There was a large stone bar-b-que pit in this commons area. One summer a dozen or so children were gathered around the pit roasting marshmallows. Now there is a real skill to roasting a marshmallow just right. Some folks like to burn the heck out of the poor sugary concoctions, but then there are those of us who are patient and gently coax a golden shell to develop around a gooey center. Perfection is when you are able to find just the right stick that will allow you to roast two marshmallows at the same time and bring both to their golden glory. I may have only been six or seven, but I understood the fine art of creating the perfect roasted marshmallow. On the day in question, some of the children were a little more aggressive than normal and I ended up being shoved. This caused my stick to lunge into the fire and naturally my marshmallows began to burn. I quickly pulled them out and blew on them to put them out, but something very unexpected happened, the sudden change of temperature caused the marshmallows to explode and the molten mass splattered onto my cheek. At that tender age I was panicked and just knew that my face would be permanently scarred. Luckily there was an adult around who put cold water on my face and got me to my parents. Needless to say, I spent the rest of the day being tended to and pampered. Children are wonderfully resilient and amazingly enough, I bare no permanent scars from that experience. What was clear was that Truman and I were no longer allowed to go to the "pit" alone. Truman was pretty steamed about that, but he eventually forgave me when my parents allowed him to venture out on his own, but did not allow me. Of course being the independent soul that I was, I felt that that was totally unfair. After all, I was just as capable as my brother—in my own mind.

I believe that those early vacations in the northern Wisconsin woods played an important role in my decision to become a biologist. My love of nature and fascination with the living organisms around me fueled my curiosity and desire to know more. I do not know if I was always asking questions, but fairly early on, I wanted to know more. My mother and my teachers must have been amazingly patient people. There is also something in my being that is at peace when I am in a wooded wilderness. When I first visited my friend's cabin in the woods in Eastern Virginia there was a remarkable transformation that took place the instant I drove from the rutted drive in the field into the wooded area. One deep inhalation and tensions of too many 80-hour weeks began to melt away, as if some invisible magnet was drawing the tensions out of my body.

2

Out of the City

The earliest memories I have are when we were still living in my birth city, Chicago, we lived at 79th and Princeton. In the late 1940's this was still a reasonably good neighborhood in which to raise families, but the neighborhood was beginning to change. I have vague, shadowy memories of my parents talking about moving to the suburbs, but there was one event that accelerated that decision significantly.

My brother has always been, even to this day, my hero. As is usually the case, the big brother tends to look out for his little sister and that seemed to be the case with us. If I was with my brother, I knew I was safe, I have seen this with my own two children as well as with other families. When Truman went "away" to school, that was traumatic for me. No longer was he there to play with me each day. Even so, he seemed to enjoy the big boy responsibility of walking to his elementary school and all the things that went on while he was gone.

Each day I would eagerly await his return from school. I recall some bay windows in the front of our flat. I would crawl behind the lace curtains and watch and wait. One day I saw something that has stuck with me throughout my life. Truman was walking home, I could see him and I know my heart tripped a beat when he came into view. I could not wait to be with him again and to hear what all had happened while he was away. Suddenly a group of older boys jumped out of the shadows and began to push and shove Truman. I did not understand why they were doing this to my brother. One of the bigger boys grabbed my brother's arm and twisted it behind him. I don't know if Truman screamed, but I did. I ran to get my mother and told her what was happening. She told me to stay put in the house, away from the windows as she ran out of the house.

The boys had wanted my brother's toy and in the process, had broken his arm. I do not recall the trip to the doctor or hospital, though I know that happened, since Truman ended up with a cast. What I do recall is that shortly thereafter we began the process of building a home in the suburbs.

In 1949, Sears Roebuck & Co. manufactured homes, in reality they sold kits. You could actually look in the catalog and select a style. Mom and Dad selected a three-bedroom home with kitchen, dining room, living room, one bathroom, a basement and a garage. It was modest, but it was to be built on a one-acre plot of land. I am not sure how they found the property, but they selected a narrow acre of land at 4440 Seeley Avenue in the little village of Downers Grove, IL., population 8,000. I suppose because it was only a block from route 34 and dad could drive into Chicago to work, Seeley Avenue was an attractive location. The land was three long blocks from the nearest elementary school, but that was a reasonable walk for my brother and me. By the time I entered third grade a new elementary school had been built down the hill from my home, less than a block away.

North of our lot was a very ancient home with ancient inhabitants who owned goats! I could not believe it, we were moving to a farm, or so it seemed to a four year old. The property was bordered on the west by a huge, untended field. On the south was a yellow brick home that seemed very sterile and on the east, across the street was the home of the founder of the community, the Pierce Downer Home. At that point in time it was not being maintained as an Historic Registry home.

The second most vivid early childhood memory that I have is one very cold February day when we went out to see how the house was progressing. It seemed like a very long ride from Chicago to Downers Grove. When we arrived at the home I was stunned, it did not look at all like the picture in the Sears and Roebuck catalog. I expected to see white siding and green shutters, grass growing, everything just like the picture. After all, when you ordered a toy from the catalog, it arrived looking just like the picture. What was before me was bare earth, 2x4's sticking into the air capped by sticks that looked like they would one day be the roof–where was the bathroom? The trip had been long and as soon as I stepped from the warm car to the cold air, I thought I would explode. My parents were so excited about their new home that they really did not want to pay attention to my pleas to find a bathroom. At age four, I learned just how uneven life is for boys and girls. Truman was able to go to the back yard and find a bush and, in relative privacy, relieve his bladder, I on the other hand had to basically strip in public so that I could relieve myself–it just was not fair!

Given the traumatic introduction to our first true home, it was amazing that I came to love it so much. It did not take long to discover that living on Seeley Avenue was great in the winter–if you were a kid. The next block south of us had a long steep hill. If there was snow, it was difficult to drive up the hill, but it was the absolute best to slide down. We would fly down the hill. After your turn you stood guard at the bottom, watching for cars until the next sledder came down. Trudging up the hill was a challenge, but it was worth the thrill.

The house would undergo several modifications over the years, but it was a wonderful place to grow up. Only a few years into the ownership of the home, the relatively unused space over the basement stairwell became a cutout and I took over that small bedroom where my bed was placed into the cutout. My brother had originally occupied the room, but it was quickly determined that it was not big enough for him, so my dolls and I were move in. I loved the bed in the wall. Tucked away at one end were some shelves where I could house my dolls and imaginary play friends. Truman even regretted, a bit, giving up the unique space. From time to time he would come in to play.

My father was good with his hands. While his day job was to be a manager with a business in Chicago, he truly enjoyed building things. The construction of the tucked away bed he did with the help of my brother. Girls were not supposed to do construction "stuff" but I was allowed to be a 'gofer' and to watch. It is amazing what I was able to learn about construction, plumbing and electrical work by watching. They are lessons that have served me very well as an adult. I even know how to read construction blueprints, something that just amazes my Chief Operating Officer today. It is a skill that I use every time my institution engages in construction projects.

My mother quickly realized that there was not enough closet space in the home, and she convinced my father to construct a wall of sliding door closets in each bedroom. Of course that reduced the size of each bedroom by a few feet, but the extra closet space was worth it. The one thing that this development did was to create a very interesting space in my parents' closet. In the initial construction, their bedroom was the only bedroom with a large closet that had sliding doors. When Dad built the new closet in their room, he built over the existing closet.

This meant that there was a hidden closet behind their clothes. For the most part they used this as storage for their off season clothes. Mom would also hide Christmas presents in that closet. What my mother did not understand was that was my favorite hiding place. I knew no one else would find me on those occasions when I wanted to get away from everyone. I admit it, I was one of those terrible kids who just could not wait until Christmas to know what I was getting. I got to be very skilled at removing Scotch Tape without ruining the paper. (And yes, I do still flip to the end of a novel to see how the story ends.)

As I moved into those difficult, hormone roller coaster years of middle school, it was clear that my room was too small for my things and it was equally clear that we needed another bathroom. One bathroom was just not enough for two adults, one teenager and one want-to-be teenager. Roughly six years after moving in, my parents began the process of building an addition to the back of the house. The plan was to expand the kitchen into my bedroom (the custom refrigerator would go in the space where my bed had been). An opening to a storage hallway would be made and then a large master bedroom suite with bathroom and dressing room would be constructed. Much of the addition was completed before they broke through my bedroom wall; that way my parents could move into the addition immediately and I moved into their bedroom.

The other important addition to the house was a basketball pole and backboard in the driveway for my brother. He was tall and basketball would become an important part of his early years.

Outside, there was a wonderful yard that developed over the years. When we moved in, there was a full, old apple tree in the front yard as well as a pear tree. Near the front corner of the house was a beautiful sugar maple tree. The back yard, however was initially devoid of any trees. In the early years Dad would mow only part of the back yard, but as the years progressed and Truman wanted more space to play, Dad mowed all the way back to the property line. We did plant a cherry tree and a weeping willow. Both would become very favorite trees for me.

Little boys were expected to climb trees, but little girls were definitely not expected to do so. Even so, I got to be pretty good at climbing trees. The apple tree was the easiest to climb since it had two very sturdy branches that were low enough for me to reach. The pear was second in ease of climbing, but eventually Dad took off the lower limbs and finally the whole tree had to be removed when the city came through with sidewalks. Truth be told, the cherry tree was the very easiest tree to climb, but it was not sturdy enough to hold our weight. Since both my brother and I loved to eat the cherries, we did not want to damage that precious tree.

Mr. and Mrs. King lived in the ancient home to the north of us. The goats made a lot of noise and smelled terribly. Even so, they fascinated and terrified me. I would go to the fence and try to get them to come to the fence so I could pet them. The Billy Goat was pretty mean and would charge me from time to time. I would run, but always come back to watch them as they chewed on their food. I do not know if my parents complained, but eventually the goats disappeared and were replaced with chickens. We even had a chicken coop for a short period of time. I wish I knew more about the Kings, but they kept to themselves. Quite frankly, the children in the neighborhood had all sorts of scary stories about them, but I suspect they were just old and tired of children. I do not recall seeing any of their own children come to visit except perhaps once or twice and that was only for the day.

On the north side of the King's property (their plot was twice as wide as ours) was a wonderful old mulberry tree. It too was a wonderful climber and the taste of the berries that were just a day or two short of full ripe still causes my mouth to water–sweet and tart. There was no way I could try and lie to my mother as to where I had been if I had been in the mulberry tree. My face, hands, top, shorts and shoes would all be stained with royal purple mulberry juice. Climbing the tree, however took some doing. The Kings did not like the kids coming and picking their mulberries, so we had to always watch to see when they were in. (When I lived in Indiana as an adult, we too had a mulberry tree in the back yard and each year I would make wonderful mulberry preserves.) The one thing we never did was to venture into the cornfield behind the King home. We knew there would be no escaping if we got caught there!

I do not know if Mr. King died and the estate sold the home, but I do recall that it was empty for a while and then finally a family with a special needs child moved in. Jimmy was a very happy child. He may have had Downs Syndrome (trisomy 21), but whatever his condition, Jimmy was pretty much kept in his yard. I remember his mother commenting about how strong Jimmy was and there was more than a little fear in her voice. In any event, Jimmy's parents were much more agreeable to our climbing their mulberry tree. They also tore down the old goat shed and chicken coop. Slowly that home began to metamorphose into a bit more modern structure.

I have not been back to the old house in many years, but the last time I was there the Pierce Downer home had been transformed into a beautiful historic building and my old home was looking pretty good.

3

Seeley Avenue Theatre

In our block of Seeley Avenue there were a number of children my age and younger. There were even some older siblings who had moved out of the nest, but were seen from time-to-time. My brother had to go two blocks to find boys his age to play with, but for me there was Betsy, Janet, and Renee. Janet Holly lived across the street and two doors down. Hers was a strange family with lots of mystery. Even so, Janet was a petite, scrappy girl who was brilliant. In spite of her tomboy looks, she was amazingly creative and she would write plays for everyone. Each summer we would hang a rope between the two pillars of her back porch. Over the rope we would fasten blankets and sheets to create our curtain. Chairs were set up immediately in front of the porch for all the neighbors to have a seat. Of course we charged a small admission fee and we had lemonade for sale as well. The setting was perfect. Two large evergreens bracketed the corners of the stage and shaded the back yard. As a result, those on stage as well as those in the audience were relatively comfortable temperature wise and the players had a "blind" from which we could wait in the wings for our entrance.

I wish I could remember what most of the plays were about, but alas, I cannot. I do know that we talked my brother and Johnny Quick (Betsy's younger brother) into participating in several of the plays. My parents, Mrs. Holly, and the Brubackers (Renee's parents) were regular attendees. From time-to-time the Quicks would come as well.

This was an environment where every child was valued and included. Betsy and I were a little chubby, but unlike at school, our neighborhood friends accepted us as we were. We both had parts in the plays. Naturally Janet had the more substantial parts, since she wrote the plays, but it really was a community effort. Everyone brought props and lemonade from home to make the evening a success.

Renee Brubacker was a tall, slender girl, probably a year older than Betsy and me, Janet might have been one year younger that me. Renee was really into ballet. She had been taking classes for some time before moving into the neighborhood. She had the kind of feet made for dancing–long and slender, with gnarled toes from going en pointe. I was totally impressed and wanted to take ballet lesions too. I was NOT tall and slender and my feet were flat. I made it through the early stages of dance class, but only made it one-year en pointe. My flat feet and chubby body just were not made for the elegance of ballet. I am quite sure that the teacher sighed a sigh of relief when I finally quit. I did not like to practice, which meant that I did not always learn the choreography for our performances until the last moment. I never embarrassed the teacher, or myself but it was doubtful until the last minute. I still love to dance, but ballet is something that I have to enjoy as a spectator, rather than a participant.

Renee was the neighborhood dancer and one time she had this idea that she and I should put on a dance recital. We did not have money for costumes, but we were able to save our allowances to buy lipstick red crape paper from which we fashioned two costumes. The skirts were okay and stayed in place, but Renee had this idea of just making a bandeau top out of a folded length of crape paper and just tie it in the back. That was okay for her, but my length of crape paper was stretched to make it around my chubby body. Definitely a recipe for disaster.

The afternoon arrived and we were in my back yard. Our stage was to be the top of the picnic table and the tape of the music, "Mares Eat Oats….," was cued on the battery powered tape player. The neighbors were there, the music started and Renee and I began our routine. Everything was fine until I inhaled more vigorously than normal. Crape paper can only stretch so much before it tears and my top tore with an explosive pop. I had all I could do to catch the strip of paper before it flew away. For a few seconds I tried to be a trouper and let the "show go on," holding my top in place with my arms clamped against my body, but the hoops and hollers from the little boys in the group were too much for me–I fled into the safety of my home, leaving Renee to go on without me. That was the last time Renee and I collaborated on any project.

Betsy and I probably spent the most amount of time together. Betsy lived in the Pierce Downer home, Pierce Downer being the founder of the village of Downers Grove. The house seemed to be in a perpetual state of renovation. It was nonetheless a happy, noisy home. Part of the time we would play at her home and part of the time we would play at mine. Betsy liked to come to my house because it was always quiet and orderly, and I always welcomed an infusion of chaos and noise that came from playing at her home. Ours was a friendship that would survive through our elementary years and part of middle school, but time and different interests seemed to take us on different paths. I wonder where she is now and what she is doing.

Betsy was my partner in crime in the only truly naughty thing I ever did in school. You see I was one of those boring "goody two shoes." I really did not experiment or do anything that was not by the book, except in kindergarten. Our kindergarten teacher was not a happy person. To those of us who were only five years old, she seemed ancient. She was a large woman who always dressed in dark dresses. I am convinced that her favorite time of the school day, second only to when we left, was naptime. Every child had to bring a little mat or rug to school, upon which we would take our "naps." Now I have never been one to take naps, even as a child, my mind just does not slow down in the middle of the day, but in kindergarten I tried to behave. One day, however, I had had enough of this ogre of a teacher. I managed to commandeer a piece of chalk. When it was time for our naps, Betsy and I strategically placed our mats right near the corner of the teacher's desk. Betsy and I took turns drawing pictures of the mean teacher under her desk. Each day, when we came to school we would glance at the floor under her desk. It took weeks before the janitors actually cleaned the floor (does that tell you how healthy it was for us to be lying on that floor?) While it was not a really bad thing to do, there was a wonderful thrill of having been able to express our dislike of this woman and to have that displeasure remain for a period of time. We were so clever, however, that I do not think even our fellow kindergarteners noticed the drawings or understood the nature of our protest. We were just ahead of our times. Having exercised my right to protest at an early age, I never did get into the protests of the 60's and 70's.

The summers were filled with a sense of freedom. Because our little block was relatively quiet, each of the children was free to roam back and forth across the street. Strangely enough, we did not venture south of my house nor did we include the children who would eventually move in north of the King's home or even further north in the block. As I reflect on that as an adult, I know there were some parental constraints put on those children that kept them from joining in with the play. The Greenwoods lived two houses south of our home, on the corner of the block. There were two boys, one a year younger and one a year older than my brother. For some reason, that friendship never developed.

As scary as the King's house was to the north, the house immediately to the south became even more frightening for me. There was a couple with a son who lived in the home. I recall hearing comments about the fact that the parents would walk around the house naked all the time. I cannot say that I ever saw that, but yes, I did look out my window more than once to see if that was true. After the couple moved in, they really kept to themselves, but several years after being in the neighborhood, they invited me to come to their back yard and even into their enclosed back porch. Inside the back porch was an early version of a hot tub. There was a brick tank that was relatively small, maybe 4'x6' but it was also fairly deep. They invited me to come in and enjoy the pool, but I declined. Later that summer of 1955, the boy invited me to join him in his tent set up in their back yard. I noticed that the father was hanging around and sort of encouraging Johnny as he lured me into the tent. Before I say more, I have to preface my comments with the fact that children in 1955 were children. At 10, I was as innocent and naive as could be. Unlike children of today who are constantly exposed to sexual themes, I still believed in the stork! Evidently Johnny's dad was hoping to turn his 13-year-old son into a man that day—at my expense. Thankfully Johnny did not exactly understand the basics, like the need for an erection. Once I was able to take back my shorts, I ran home. I did not know what to say to my mother. I knew something wrong happened, but I was not hurt, just embarrassed. When I finally was able to formulate some words and try and explain, my mother fell apart. I did not understand what terrible thing I had done–after all, my brother and I had seen each other naked before, but she filled the tub with hot, hot water and made me sit in it for what seemed an eternity.

My father came home and I know he was angry and I know he went to see the neighbors, but nothing seemed to happen except we did not talk with them any more and I was told to never go near them. From that point on, my mother would subtly tell me what some men are really like (in her opinion). Everything was veiled in implications and nothing was clear. This early trauma and subsequent brainwashing was to have an impact on me for many years. Growing up in an era where sexual matters were never discussed made it difficult to understand what my body was telling me, versus what my mother had told me. Thank heavens I became a biologist and began to understand the facts of life, not the Victorian myths.

4

The Adventurer

I developed an adventuresome spirit fairly early on. While I preferred having my big brother around, he was nowhere near as happy to have me tagging along, so out of necessity I would explore on my own. Two of my adventures had varying degrees of success, but both were to portend the risk-taking woman who would emerge from the cocoon of childhood.

The summer adventure was not the most successful, but certainly garnered the greatest degree of attention and subsequent discipline. I was always interested in the vegetation in my yard as well as the insects and animals that would wander through from time to time. We were suburban dwellers, not rural dwellers, so the fauna was limited to squirrels, insects, rabbits and stray dogs and cats (save the goats and chickens from next door.) One summer evening my brother was having his cub scout meeting at our home. I was told that, under no circumstance was I allowed to intrude on this sacred meeting. Mom was busy preparing snacks, Dad was one of the scoutmasters and Truman was of course the star of the troupe. That meant that I was on my own. I was probably 5 at the oldest. At that age many children are interested in fire. Since the scouts were talking about how to build good campfires, and since I was not allowed to join them, I decided to show them up (some of my adult friends would say that I have not changed.) I found a box of kitchen matches and headed for the field behind our property. It was a beautiful sunny early evening and the insects were out in droves. I decided to set up my mini camp (I did have a glass of water with me to be safe) in the weeds. I pulled some of the long grass to make a clear area and then sat down to watch the grasshoppers. I was fascinated with their coming and going and how their legs worked.

When I had had my fill of belly button biology, I decided to gather my materials for my fire. I did not want a big fire because that could be dangerous, but just a little one would do. I took some of the grasses that I had pulled and made a little pile of them. Then with care, I lit one of the kitchen matches. There was a breeze, so the first match blew out, as did the second and the third. I was determined, however and on the forth try, my match stayed lit and I held it to the edge of the pile of grass. Given that I was trying to light fresh grass, things did not burn very easily. In fact there was far more smoke than anything. I had to move to avoid getting smoke in my eyes.

My mother was in the kitchen preparing the snack for the boys and happened to look out the kitchen window. What she saw mortified her—one blonde curly head of hair in the weeds and lots of smoke. She sounded the alarm to my father and the scouts. Everyone came screaming out to the field. No one seemed to understand that I had things under control, or so I thought. I had my water and was just about to put the fire out. That evening I learned about another kind of fire—one that did not allow me to sit for two days. My parents had never been that much into corporal punishment, but that night they wanted to make a point, boy did they ever!!!

My next grand adventure came either that winter or the following winter and was the most daring of my young life. Roughly three blocks west of my home, where Grant Street ended, was an overgrown region with a small stream running through it. I had seen it a few times when we would drive that way to pick up one of Truman's friends. As a biologist, I now know that this area was a secondary, riparian succession region. The trees in the area were all small and there were many woody plants–all indications that this area had been cleared at some point and then allowed to grow wild. For a 6 year old, however, it was just the right size jungle, albeit a winter jungle. Since there were no massive trees, one could see fairly far into the overgrowth and I felt that it was a place I could go to explore without getting lost.

There was plenty of snow on the ground on this day. I told my mother I was going to play outside, but wanted to know if I could take a thermos of hot choc-olate with me. Amazingly she agreed without asking too many questions. Hot chocolate made and stored in the thermos, I bundled up in my winter overalls, jacket, hat, gloves, snow boots and scarf. I also put a drawing tablet, some pencils and some crackers in a paper bag. In the garage was my snow sled. This was a real sled, not a plastic sheet, but the old wooden sled with metal runners. There was already a rope tied to the crossbars so I loaded my treasures onto the sled and began my walk toward the great adventure. Down the street past the two houses and then turned right. About one or one and a half blocks down Grant Street I was beginning to doubt the wisdom of pulling the sled. It never seemed this long when riding in the car.

For my short little legs the new snow was deep and heavy and the sled pulled me backwards. I finally stopped by the side of the street to rest for a little while. Energized, I forded ahead. Soon I could see the end of the road and the forest ahead. Success was within my grasp. The weeds were fairly thick on the edge of the woods, but I found a region that I could pull my sled through. I knew there was a creek nearby and so I headed deeper into the woods. Finally I could see the depression where the water trickled by. The wind picked up and I was getting cold. Having read about adventurers, I knew it was possible to build a lean-to to cut down the wind, but how? I did not bring any matches to start a fire–my sum-mer experience nixed that!! I looked around and found a few fallen branches, gathering them I leaned them against one another forming a teepee like shape. There was one pine tree fairly near by my campsite and I was able to break off two small, lower branches. By leaning these branches against the "teepee" I was able to cut down the wind a bit. I backed the sled as close to my enclosure as possible, sat on the sled and drank my hot chocolate.

I am not sure how long I stayed in my little campground, but the blissful silence was only interrupted now and then by the sound of a hardy bird. I can still remember the sense of absolute silence. It was both thrilling and a little frightening. I really was far away from civilization. As is usually the case with children, stories abounded about this region and the wild animals that roamed the woods. I was not sure that those stories were true, but the silence tended to assure me that nothing was lurking about. Nonetheless, I did peek around my blind from time-to-time to be sure nothing was creeping up on me.

Once the hot chocolate was gone and I had drawn a few pictures, I knew I needed to head home. I was cold and the sun was not shining as brightly as it had when I set out on my adventure. I imagined that my mother was probably getting worried about my where-abouts. Do you know how far three blocks are when you are cold and tired and six years old? Getting out of the woods was easy, but it seemed like Grant Street continued to grow longer and longer the more I walked and pulled my sled behind me. One of the most blessed sights was the sight of my brother coming down Grant Street towards me. He had been sent out to look for me and noticed the sled marks (see, he learned something in scouts.) I am not sure I was ever so glad to see anyone, as I was to see him. He took my hand and the rope from the sled and together we made it home. Big brothers are life savers!! My mother was not too happy that I was exploring down Grant Street, but she never knew just how far down Grant Street I had ventured. Years later, as a teenager I went for a walk and ended up at my woods. I was totally stunned to see a tiny lean-to in the middle of the woods. Some things we build can last a long time, guess we better do it right.

5

Footprints in My Life

Besides our parents, it is clear that from time-to-time a person will come into our lives and leave an indelible imprint on our hearts. As an adult there have been several wonderful people who have done just that, but there are those who were present in my formative years who have had a life long impact on me. Uncle · Tutee was one of those who walked all over my heart–in the most positive of senses. To the children in his Chicago, Lincoln Park neighborhood, he was Uncle Tutee. He was wonderful at slight of hand tricks and could make a quarter appear from the most unusual of places on the child's head. Sometimes it was a book of matches that just slid out of one's ear and you never felt it coming out. You always knew you were going to have a delightful time in his presence. For me, however, he was Granddad. In actuality, he was not my biological grandfather, but he was my "real" grandfather. Helen Kingston Dibos did abandon my mother shortly after my mother was born–leaving her to be raised by Helen's parents. It was my mother's understanding that her father died before she was born. Helen took off and was not to be heard from again until sometime in the early 1940's (my mother was born in 1910.) It appears that Helen married a man who discovered that the woman he married had a daughter and that daughter had a child or two. He had always wanted to be father. If he could not be a father, then a grandfather was just fine. Because of his love of children, he insisted on being a part of our lives.

Trips into Chicago were always tense. I know that my mother did not talk with Grandma very much, but I was always too busy playing with Granddad to worry about it. Grandma rarely interacted with my brother and me, but it was a constant love-fest with Granddad. Granddad also had a brother and sister who were fascinating because they both spoke with a rich German accent, though my granddad did not. The explanation was that they came to America when my grandfather was very young, but being the older siblings, their primary language was German. I did not see them often, but usually at Christmas time Helena and Alfred would appear. They were not as entertaining as Granddad, but because they were exotic, they were very interesting.

It was clear, even in advanced age, that my grandfather was the baby of his family. His siblings would tease and chide him like any older sibling might, but they also had a great deal of respect for him as well. I never heard them contradict my grandfather. The family dynamic was very interesting. I did not think too much about it as a child or teen, but as an adult I now have to wonder.

Granddad led a most fascinating life as a young man. As a teenager he was paid to dive off the bridge into the Chicago River each Sunday as part of the summer picnics in the park. Given the condition of the Chicago River today, you could not find enough money to get someone to do that now. As Albert Dibos aged, his life became even more colorful. During Prohibition he ran a speakeasy and even later in his life he ran book. There are times when I wonder if the beautiful diamond ring that I wear today, that used to be on his finger all the time, was not a pay-off for some bet! He would tease us with stories, but he never revealed too much about his life. Perhaps it was a good thing that we did not know more.

I do not know what their source of income was. I know that my grandmother would periodically take us to Berghoff's on Adams Street in Chicago. That was always (and still is) a favorite restaurant for my brother and myself. The food was excellent, but the ambience was even better. During those trips my grandfather would not be present and I never knew where he was. Grandma would always say that it was her time with us, though clearly she was uncomfortable with us, and Granddad was busy. This may be one time where ignorance is bliss. One thing that made Berghoff's so special has to do with its history. The restaurant first opened in Ft. Wayne, IN in 1887 and then expanded to Chicago in 1898. The founders were immigrants from Germany and once they got the Chicago restaurant and brewery going, they hired only German waiters. When a waiter would come in in the morning, they would buy tokens from the kitchen. As a customer you would purchase your meal from the waiter at the published price, his take home was the difference between what he paid the kitchen and what you paid him. The waiters did not have "stations" to work, they worked the entire restaurant. This meant that there was competition between waiters and it also meant that the waiters were hustling as fast as they could. The challenge for my brother and me was to get them to slow down enough to make them smile. Not surprisingly, the private entrepreneur concept did not last much past the early 1950's.

My grandfather always sang to me singing that he would dance at my wedding. We even practiced over the years. Sadly, Granddad died 33 days before that wedding—he was definitely missed. Even today, I realize that I have no pictures of my grandfather, only one with my grandmother.

How can someone leave footprints on your heart and soul when you have never met them? Ella Phillips knew just how to do that. Between the end of the nineteenth century and 1917, Ella and Wilbur Phillips gave birth to ten children. Wilbur was a brilliant speech writer, but had participated in the Spanish American war. During the war he sustained a head injury and the family believes that the injury was responsible for periodic violent outbursts. In order to not hurt anyone, Wilbur would disappear for periods of time. One has only to look at a photo of the ten Phillips children to know he was home at least ten times.

Ella was ahead of her time; a nurse who worked with the Salvation Army, she was always helping others through difficult times. Rather than looking for a handout, Ella and her ten were always there to offer a hand-up to those less fortunate. The Phillips clan did not bemoan what they did not have, rather they celebrated what they did have and found ways to reach out and help others. In the middle of that pack of ten was George Truman Phillips, my father. All ten of the children stayed close throughout their lifetimes. From the ten came 17 children who likewise have stayed close though we are scattered across the globe.

What kinds of footprints did Ella leave on my heart? Though she died before I was born, through her children she taught me the importance of living possibilities, not bemoaning missed gifts. This was a lesson that would be essential as I grew into my profession. She taught me the importance of giving to others. And she taught me about unconditional love. Though her son did not offer me that unconditional love, his siblings did. I am so glad they learned the lesson. Finally she taught me the importance of family. There is such love in the Phillips family. All but one of the original ten are gone now and the remaining sibling mentally is not with us any longer. Even so, the cousins are a constant source of support and love for each other.

A few years back one of my cousins, Eddie decided to go back to school and get his PhD–this at age 60+. He had retired from the Navy and then from United Airlines, but he was anything but retiring! About half way through the program he was diagnosed with non-Hodgkins Lymphoma. The family rallied around him and we all celebrated when he defeated the disease. At about age 63 he received his diploma and is now teaching at Southern Illinois University and is still participating in Iron Man competitions. I am proud of you Eddie. As he was considering going back to school, Eddie would communicate with me, and I suspect my brother, to see what it was like to get our doctorates. I tried to offer him encouragement as he progressed through the program. Getting one's doctorate is really like jumping through a series of hoops, you just have to keep at it–there is an end point.

Imagine being surrounded by dozens of talkative (yes, I do mean loud,) opinionated, loving, hugging people if your only family experience had been with very distant people. During my 22-year marriage, my husband was very uncomfortable with the large Phillips clan. Seventy to a hundred folks milling around all talking, all with an opinion and probably all sandwiched into the kitchen can be rather daunting. The sad thing was that he could not see the love that flowed through the group and as a result, we pulled away from family gatherings. I stayed in touch through the "dreaded" Christmas letter lovingly know as the Philklan News. I even edited the paper for many years in the 80's, but the summer our divorce was finalized there was a cousins' reunion. I took my children up to Michigan to the event and it was as if we had never been away, the unconditional love flowed from everyone. We have not missed a reunion since then. The beauty of this family is that the next generation has now taken up the mantle and plans the reunions and edits the Christmas letter. My daughter was the first of the next generation to single handedly take over running the reunion, though one of her cousins, working with her parents, was substantially responsible for the reunion that preceded the Colorado reunion. What a joy to see that the next generation "gets it." They understand the importance of the extended family and the power that that foundation has for their lives.

There are others who have left an imprint on my heart and they will float in and out of my stories, but I would be remiss to not mention my two children. Both are extremely bright (spoken not only as mother, but as an educator) and both have become wonderful, successful adults. They are unique personalities, and no parent could be more proud of the adults they have become, I love them dearly. For the most part, we can talk about anything and they are learning to trust me as an adult, rather than as a parent. When I think about the family situations for many acquaintances, I know I am blessed to have Ryan and Nicole as my own.

6

Those Who Can, Teach

In the 1970's there was a phrase out that rankled every educator, it said, "those who can't, teach". The assumption was that you only went into teaching because you did not have the academic ability to succeed in something else. As a counterpoint, Kevin Ryan wrote a book entitled, *Those Who Can, Teach*. The book is now in its tenth edition and is a must for anyone considering teaching as a profession.

It has always amazed me that when you ask people their impressions of teachers, there is still a sense that only those who cannot make it elsewhere choose teaching. But ask them about their favorite teachers, the ones who made a difference in their lives–and there always are examples–they know that those individuals were born to teach and they were very gifted at what they did. The distain for teachers does not include their own teachers. The disconnect is difficult for most to see, which makes the attitude about teachers in general a difficult prejudice to overcome.

There have been teachers over the years who have had a profound impact on my life, most positive, a few negative. I would like to think that there are more than a few former students in the world who put me into the positive impact category.

I already shared with you the story of my kindergarten teacher. I do not recall her name, but I recall her severe nature. That was to become a reverse model for me. When I finally settled on teaching, I knew I wanted to be a positive role model rather than a negative one.

My first really positive teacher was a third grade teacher by the name of Miss Cinnamon. I loved the spice, and I loved her name. She was an amazing combination of cool detachment and intense interest in the individual. Miss Cinnamon was always fair. I rarely got into trouble in class, because I wanted her to be proud of me. If I did something I should not, the fact that she was upset with me was more the punishment than the actual metered out punishment. One time I forgot something at home and ran up the steep hill behind the school, through the Quick's yard and across the street to my home. I did this during recess and was back before recess was over, but Miss Cinnamon saw me through the classroom window. The school rule was that you did not leave the schoolyard. Because the schoolyard was almost an extension of my home, I did not think it would be a problem. Wrong!! I had to stay after school that day. I apologized profusely, was forgiven and then was allowed to help with some of the set up for the next day's classes.

Miss Cinnamon was a slender woman of indeterminate age. Her jet-black hair was pulled back in a severe bun, but she often selected very fashionable dresses. It was not unusual to see her dressed in a red suit or a red polka dot dress. She tended towards being quiet, but there was always kindness in her voice. I do not know what Miss Cinnamon saw in me, but she detected a potential and she fostered that potential. By the end of third grade, I had decided I wanted to be a teacher.

My love of science, however just could not be suppressed. Every opportunity we had to conduct and experiment, I was front and center. If there was a project to survey the organisms in our playground, I was on my hands and knees counting. When I entered 5th grade Mrs. Gaunt who was a young, first year teacher, picked up on my love of science and shared with me that her husband was a nuclear physicist. Better yet, he worked at Argonne National Laboratory. She and her husband arranged for me to pay him a visit at his laboratory. I am surprised that my eyeballs are not still somewhere on the floors of Argonne, I was dazzled. I still recall the smells and sounds of the vast Argonne research areas. I did not quite understand what a nuclear physicist did, but my fate was set–I was bound to become a scientist. While I was good at mathematics, it seemed to me that physics was a pretty lonely discipline. Being a more social person, I gravitated to biochemistry then to biology and finally a degree in both biology and chemistry with a post-doc in protein biochemistry. It was not until my senior year in high school that I decided I wanted to move into science teaching. One person is responsible for that decision, Dr. Robert Dorsey at Franklin Township High School.

Bob Dorsey was the ultimate science teacher. I had just moved to New Jersey for my senior year and though he did not know me, he saw a potential in me and began to develop that potential. I can still remember my amazement the day he allowed me to do a make-up test in his prep room without anyone being present. That level of trust was just unheard of in my previous experiences, but Mr. Dorsey trusted me. I was not about to take advantage of that trust.

It was in Bob Dorsey's Advanced Biology course where all that I had been learning began to come together and make sense. I could see the interplay of chemistry, mathematics and even physics with biology. Things that happen in a living organism began to make sense and the different biochemical pathways in our bodies all had a purpose and were all interconnected. I wanted to be able to turn on the light bulb for students the way Mr. Dorsey did for me.

Mr. Dorsey was not afraid to let the students see the human side of him either. He had a growing family and around the time I was in his class, his wife gave birth to triplets, making it a total of six children—all boys. They continued to try, and I understand they finally had a little girl some years later. While Mr. Dorsey was teaching us, he was completing his doctoral studies and eventually went on to teach at, what then was known as, Douglass College for Women, in New Brunswick, NJ.

Mr. Dorsey also got me my first summer job—that of lifeguard at a Raritan Valley County Club, Somerville, NJ. I have always loved the water and being a lifeguard was an ideal job. I was to continue that job through college until my graduation. Eventually I moved up to head lifeguard and swim team coach. We had some wonderful swimmers and some great kids with a great heart for the sport. I still have the massive silver meat platter and the white gold watch that the teams gave to me after each winning season. They serve to remind me just how important hard work and a positive attitude are, because those are the things that made our teams winners. Sure there was talent, but without the work and heart, talent fails.

Lurking in the back of my mind was the fact that I wanted to be a doctor, but in the early 1960's in the midwestern mindset, that just was not something a woman did. Wanting to be a teacher or nurse was fine, but.... Since my father was the most discouraging about medicine, and since I was always trying to gain his approval, I gave up the idea of becoming a doctor. The negative view on medicine was a very subtle push against succeeding, but there was to be a very blatant slam against my wanting to be in the sciences that was to come my sophomore year at Purdue University. I loved my time at Purdue. As Indiana's Land Grant school, there was a commitment to the students and to the community. There was both an earthy quality to Purdue as well as a cutting edge research quality.

Since I was trying to get a major in both biology and chemistry along with my teaching certification, I usually carried between 19 and 22 credits each semester. My sophomore year was the time for analytical chemistry. I walked into the lecture room along with about 249 other students, all males. The professor walked into the room, he was a short, squat, balding man who now reminds me of the two, old Muppet characters in the balcony during the Muppet shows. In any event, Dr. Laskowsky looked around the room and then he saw me. He stopped dead in his tracks and said in an angry heavy accent, "I do not like 'vimen' in my class. If you are going to stay here I 'vill' tell 'vat' ever jokes I 'vant' 'vether' you like them or not!"

Here I was in the middle of a room of 250 students, I needed the course for my majors–leaving was not an option. Good to his word, Dr. Laskowsky was as crude and rude as he could possibly be. In the beginning the young men in the class laughed with the jokes, but as the weeks progressed, they stopped laughing. They understood what the professor was trying to do and they understood that it was not fair or appropriate. When the students stopped laughing, he stopped telling the jokes. I did not ace the course, but I think I managed a B out of it, thanks in great part to my fellow students. I wish I could go back in time to thank them for their support, at the time I did not realize just how significant it was. From this professor I learned how not to teach and how not to be inclusive.

Thankfully Laskowsky was an exception at Purdue. My Organic professor, Embryology professor and more, all provided model after model of what it means to be passionate about ones subject matter and passionate about others' opportunity to learn. That is a powerful combination and one I hope I was able to emulate when I was in the classroom.

It was during the summer after my freshman year at Purdue, that I decided to go into teaching. More specifically, I decided that I would get my secondary teaching license so that I could earn some money and then I would go back to school to get my doctorate so that I could teach at the college level. The fact that I could also do some research, once at the college level, was an additional incentive. My future path was set and I could not wait to see how it all unfolded.

As I read over what I have included in this chapter, I am reminded of several research efforts to look at when we need to reach young children and capture their interest in science. Most of the research tells us that a child's interest in science grows through about age 10-12 and if you are ever going to succeed in getting them into a field of science you have to do it by age 14. Clearly I followed in that pattern. By age 12 I knew I wanted to go into a scientific field, thankfully I had teachers who fostered that interest.

7

First love

Somewhere about the time we moved from Chicago to the suburbs I began to change from being an average sized child to being a chubby child. While there have been articles written about how adults mistreat overweight adults, that is nothing compared to how children treat other children who are overweight. Except for my neighborhood friends, the children at school were brutal about my size. I knew that I was capable as a student, but the taunting would affect my level of personal confidence for much of my life. Even so, I tried to be as active as I could. As my body began the transition through puberty, the weight was slow to come off, but finally my freshman year in high school the weight seemed to melt off. For the first time in more than a decade I was averaged sized. Nonetheless, I was not confident around boys. That was until I met Dave in my MYF (Methodist Youth Fellowship) group. Like me, he had spent much of his life battling his size, but when I met him he was two years older than me. He was a member of the football team and baseball team. My brother was on the football team as a tight end and Dave was the team's kicker and sometimes center.

We would often sit together during activities and soon fell into a comfortable banter that happens between friends. Finally, he asked me to the winter formal and I thought I had died and gone to heaven. I can still remember the dress my mother and I made. It was white satin, strapless and knee length. Over the satin was a sheer, pale blue embroidered "over dress" with scallops at the top and bottom. Mom also made gauntlet like gloves from the blue material. I felt like a princess when Dave gave me a wrist corsage and we drove off in his 1957 red and white Chevy Impala. Needless to say, I was in love for the first time (the guy.... and maybe the car too).

It was an innocent age. For two years we were inseparable, but given my childhood "lessons" about men, we never went beyond some serious kissing. Over the two years I got to know his younger brother and sisters and his parents. Dave's father was a pilot, so I did not see him that often and Dave's mother was definitely not excited to have me around. We spent more time at my home because I do not think she wanted me in their home.

We never seemed to run out of things to talk about and I know I had my school notebook covered with his name and probably a few hopeful, Mrs. David Smith's. Such is the way with your first time for love, albeit young love.

During the summer between my freshman and sophomore years, Dave invited me to come up to their cabin in Tomahawk, Wisconsin. A terrible bout of poison oak kept me from going up with them, but a week later I was able to take a bus up there. Here I was again in a cabin in the woods in Wisconsin. It was a wonderful home filled with laughter, sibling bickering, great aromas and just warm family stuff. Dave taught me to water ski, which was thrilling and challenging. All of the Smith's knew how to ski, so I had to do a lot to catch up with them. By week's end I was beginning to get the hang of slalom skiing–just barely.

Speaking of "barely," the most embarrassing thing that happened to me came the first day that Dave and I went out swimming. I was getting pretty good with my sewing and had made a new bathing suit for the trip. It was a white cotton piquet fabric with a red and white polka dot cummerbund. The back was cut to the waist. I thought I looked good in it and I was proud to wear it first for Dave– that was until after I got out of the water. Although I had lined the suit, I did not select a heavy enough fabric. Once wet, it was like tissue paper. Not surprisingly, Dave noticed that fact much before I did. Finally I had to ask him why he had such a funny look on his face. His stammered response sent me diving for my towel. We laughed, but I thought I would die.

More than forty years later he would place a surprise call to my office and told my administrative assistant to say that he was someone looking for someone who could make white bathing suites for 16-year-old girls, he heard I might know what he was talking about. When my administrative assistant shared this anony-mous caller's greeting I almost fell off my chair laughing. I had no doubt about the identity of the caller. It was a fun conversation with great reminiscing. We will always be friends even if we do not talk or visit for decades. Some bonds of friendship do last a lifetime.

Dave was the first one to break my heart as well. At the end of our second summer, Dave went off to college and I moved to Terre Haute, IN. Dad had been working as the plant manager for a liquor distributor in Chicago. The com-pany changed hands and the new owners wanted my father to falsify the state tax documents. My father would not do that and was subsequently dismissed. With almost a year of looking, he landed the job of plant manager for Columbia Records, division of CBS in Terre Haute, IN. For all of the 1960-61 school year he had been in Terre Haute while we tried to sell the house. Finally in the sum-mer of 1961 we moved to Indiana.

During Dave's first two months at college we wrote periodically, and he did come down for a fall dance in Terre Haute. Actually, I wrote every day and Dave's letters became less and less frequent. We had agreed to meet back up in Downers Grove for Homecoming. As my mother drove me back to Downers Grove, I was finishing the hem on my dress for the dance. The game was great and at the dance it was wonderful to be back in Dave's arms. Even so, I sensed a distance. On the drive to my friend's home he became more and more distant. As we sat in my friend's driveway, he told me that he had found someone at college and he was going to break up with me. There is only one other time in my life when I have ever cried so hard. I managed to hold on until I got out of his car, but my poor friend could not begin to understand what I was trying to say because I was sobbing so.

For the rest of my school year in Terre Haute I was like a ghost. I moved through the motions, did well academically, but socially I was in deep mourning. At the end of that school year I knew that my father had been promoted to a vice presidency with CBS and we would be moving east. That possibility of moving away from the pain jogged me out of my painful funk.

All year long one friend had been telling me that he wanted me to meet his big brother who was away at college. Jay would build up this big brother until I was convinced that he must walk on water. There was a deep love in the family, though I did not get to know the family well. Even so, I knew that Lynn was the godlike big brother. Jay was a year older than myself and then there were two or three fairly young sisters. The father was a local pastor and the family's interests centered on their church.

Finally around the time of my birthday, August 1962, the big brother came home for a short stay. At Jay's insistence, Lynn and I had our first and only date. That was all it took, I was in love once again. I was stunned that someone I just met could totally sweep me off my feet. Lynn had borrowed one of his friend's green MG to take me to the movie (I don't have a clue what we saw) and then we went to the church to check in on an activity that was going on. Finally Lynn drove me home and I thought I was being kissed for the first time. My insides turned to a quivering mass. I may have been a naïve young girl, but what I was feeling was anything but little girl-ish. I had reason to believe Lynn was affected as well. I am not sure how we did it, but the windows on the car were definitely steamed up–in August!!

For all of my senior year in high school, in New Jersey and his senior year at Indiana Central we wrote on almost a daily basis. Later in the year Lynn's letters were a bit less frequent and a little less promising of a future, but I assumed that his student teaching and getting ready to graduate were occupying his time and interests. In the fall I planned to move back to Indiana to attend Purdue University to be closer to Lynn. I was surprised that I did not hear from Lynn all that much during the summer before coming back to Indiana, but I was still in love and I believed.

Once settled into Purdue's culture I was convinced that I would have time to go to Indianapolis to visit Lynn. His brother told me that Lynn was coming to the Purdue–Notre Dame game early in the fall, so I assumed that I would see him. I waited and waited at the dorm for his "surprise" call, but it never came. Finally, before half time I headed out to the game. The next morning I understood why I had not heard from him. The Indianapolis paper had a policy of printing large color photos of the young women who were announcing their engagements. As I walked through the lobby of my dorm, the Social section was sitting on a bench. My eyes were instantly drawn to the names over one photograph. Now Lynn has a fairly unique name and it was there over this lovely looking woman's photo. With shaking hands I picked up the paper and read the epitaph of my second great love.

As with Dave, Lynn and I have been able to establish an adult friendship that has been most fulfilling. Since Lynn eventually went into higher education, I frequently called him for advice as I made my way through the maze of academe. From time-to-time we would get together for lunch and would talk about our youthful love. He is now loving his retirement, grandchildren and fishing. What a class act he was and still is.

8

College Life

In high school, even though I was moving around, I began to demonstrate some significant leadership skills. Even after moving and being the new kid on the block, I ended up being an editor for a yearbook, a class officer, etc. College was to be no different. Early in my time at Purdue University I got involve with residence hall governance. While I never ended up being the president of the residence hall, I always held one office or another.

Late in my freshman year two interesting things happened. The first thing to happen was that Dave and I reconnected. He had become the president of Cary Quad and was enjoying his popularity on campus. On one level it was like old times, we could talk about anything, but on another level I was not able to re-create that first time loving feeling. Dave had come out to New Jersey over the summer for the World's Fair, which we enjoyed considerably, but when I came back from my summer of lifeguarding, I knew that it would not work. I suspect he was a little relieved. We liked each other, but now as emerging adults, we could not create the loving bond necessary to last a lifetime.

The second thing that happened was that some men from one of the residence halls sent me a plaque that belonged to their residence hall. They wanted me to ransom it so they could come and serenade our residence hall. I called the young man, who was the president of the residence hall to suggest he bring some men over to sing for the plaque, but it was near the end of the semester and he blew it off totally.

Having a summer of lifeguarding and coaching a swimming team, I was ready to rededicate my efforts to succeeding academically as well as socially. I had not been too good at balancing the two my first year, but I knew I could make it and do well. I still had this silly plaque, so I put in one final call to this guy who ignored me the previous spring. Suddenly he was interested in coming to get the plaque. He and his roommate would talk with me on the phone for hours and finally a date was set to sing for the plaque. I will admit that the guys did a good job and I walked out of the dorm, after hours to present the plaque to the President of H-1, Joe Speece.

Not long after that evening Joe asked me go to a movie with him. Joe was a fifth year senior in Industrial Management with aspirations of going to law school. He had spent three years in Civil Engineering before deciding that was not what he wanted, nor was it where his skills were the strongest. I can remember coming home from the date and telling my roommate that I thought I had found the man I just might marry. As I write this, I am beginning to see a pattern—I guess I do fall in love fairly quickly at times. That is not always the case, but it certainly was with Lynn and to some extent with Joe. In each case, however, there had been a significant period of getting to know the other person. Dave and I had been in a youth group together for some time before we became a couple, Lynn had been built up in my mind for a year before we met and that was the closest to "love at first sight" that I had experienced at that point in time. With Joe, we had spent hours and days getting to know each other before we ever went on a date, so I suppose that does not constitute love at first sight. There would be only one other experience in my life when "love at first sight" truly did take place and I am still reeling from the experience.

Joe and I began dating in the fall of 1964. It was probably around the first of the year in 1965 when we began talking about our life together once I graduated. Joe was accepted into law school at Indiana University for the fall of 1965 and we knew we would be apart, but we felt we could make it. Joe never asked me to marry him and never gave me an engagement ring, we just moved from dating to planning a wedding. I wanted to be able to say I was engaged, but Joe did not have the funds for or believe in engagement rings, so for months I felt like I was on tender hooks. Finally, my mother prodding to put something in the paper, I pressed Joe to know if we were or were not engaged. His answer was, "yea, I guess we are." I should have been cautious, but I was in love, and I think he was as well.

My last semester at Purdue was a blur. I was hired out of my student teaching to replace a teacher (Mr. Bush) who was on an NSF (National Science Foundation) grant to teach in India. Most of my professors allowed me to take exams early and I went to work each morning at West Lafayette High School. What an experience. My fellow teachers were wonderfully supportive and helped as I finished out the school year. Anyone who has ever done substitute teaching knows the challenge the students can pose for the replacement, but since I was a real hire, rather than a sub, the students gave me a little room. Mr. Bush had been doing such wonderful things in his class before I arrived that it was an exciting position to move into.

I participated in my graduation on June 3, 1967, turned my grades in for the students at West Lafayette High School the morning of June 9, attended a rehearsal dinner that evening and on the afternoon of June 10, 1967, I walked down the aisle of the church to become Mrs. Joseph M. Speece, Jr. My mother had made my dress and my bridesmaids were in very simple linen sheaths. It was the age of simplicity. Later I would shorten my wedding dress and even wear it as a party dress in the summers. Joe's family was not comfortable at fancy parties and I was reminded how much my college had just cost my parents, so we kept things very minimal. The honeymoon was minimal as well; we spent two nights in an old Holiday Inn motel in Michigan City, IN. We spent our days on the beach of Lake Michigan. We had each other and we were happy.

Eventually we were able to move into University housing and into much more comfortable space. At the same time I got my first full-year teaching job. I became the science department at Gosport School in Gosport, IN. The ancient, brick two-story building was in terrible shape. Wooden stairs were warped, as were the wooden floors in the hallways. More than once I tripped when I did not anticipate the undulation of the floor. My teaching assignment was to teach science 7, 8, 9, biology and chemistry every day. The caveat was that I had no equipment and no supplies, oh yes, and no budget. My salary was $5290 for the year. Joe worked about two weekends a month at Sears to supplement our income, but his main focus was to make it through his last year of law school and to pass the bar exam.

I loved teaching in Gosport. It was a huge departure from my experience in the affluent West Lafayette High School, but there were some wonderful young people in my classes. One student, however was not so young. Othie Reynolds was probably as old as I was, or very nearly. A mountain of a man, Othie did not like school and most teachers did not like Othie. He drove a truck with loaded shotguns in the rack. I could not understand the teachers' dislike of Othie, he was a pussycat. Initially he tried to intimidate me, but I just was not buying it. Typically I would laugh at some of his attempts as if he had just recited the funniest joke. Pretty soon Othie realized that I was not intimidated but I was interested in his learning something. Once I called his bluff we got along wonderfully. Othie did not attend class regularly, but when he did he would have some interesting things to contribute. For that year, at least, I was able to reach Othie and he learned how to get along with the other students in the class. More than once I have wondered what ever happened to Othie. He could be running moonshine in the hills of southern Indiana or he could be the president of a corporation, who knows?

Money was tight that year, really tight. Joe's tuition costs and books, the rent and car all ate into my meager income. Finally in the late winter I knew that we could not pay some of our bills. We needed some money for groceries and the only thing I could think to do was to sell was my flute. Luckily one of my students wanted to get a better flute and she bought mine—that got us through the roughest spot. Years later I was lamenting giving up the flute, when I realized that I was being silly. I could afford to buy myself a new one and I did. Now can I play it? No way, but I do get it out from time-to-time and practice a little. More than anything, the flute represents the rich cycle of my life.

Shortly after our wedding my mother went to her doctor. She had been having some difficulties and now that her youngest was married and taken care of, she would take care of herself. The doctor indicated that they needed to operate to see what was going on inside of her. Sometime in August of 1967 they operated. It was a short operation, for when they opened her up, they realized that it was much too late–the cancer was throughout her abdominal region. She was 56 years old at the time and I was not at all ready to give up my mother. I was just beginning my adult life and I was counting on her advice and help. I wanted her to be a grandmother to my children, to teach them the wonderful things only grandmothers can teach.

Mom rallied and that winter Dad was moved to California to become the head of Fender Guitar. Mom stayed in New Jersey to once again sell the home. Because Joe and I had no money, I could not go and visit her. Shortly before Mothers Day 1968, Mom was admitted to the hospital again. I did not understand why my father was not there with her, if nothing else, why not move her to a hospital in California to be with her, but he did not–she was on her own. On Mother's Day I called the hospital to talk with her. I was not connected with her room, but with the nurse's station. The head nurse got on and literally yelled at me saying what a terrible daughter I was because I was not there with Mom. She was dying and no one was there. They had tried to reach my father and could not get to him and it was my fault. I should step back here and tell you that neither my mother nor father had shared with me the severity of Mom's condition. I knew she had surgery and was doing okay. She must have been okay if Dad moved to California without her, right? I did know that we were dealing with cancer, but I did not know the magnitude of the problem. My mother was very private and just did not share her problems with others. When the head nurse told me my mother was dying I was devastated. Of course she then immediately switched me to my mother. I was sobbing but had to quickly pull myself together to have a cheery conversation with her. She sounded weak, but happy. I told her I would come to see her as soon as I could.

I spent the remainder of the day trying to track down my father. It turns out he was staying with his sister in Laguna Beach. Within the next few days he flew back to New Jersey and then talked with both my brother and me to say that yes, Mom was likely in her final days. I quickly finished up the grades for my students and because of the kindness of several folks, was able to fly out to New Jersey. I spent several days with Mom, Truman and Dad. There were times when she knew us and she did say good-bye, in her own way. I had a flight I needed to take back to Indiana, but by the time my flight had landed, Mom's flight to heaven had taken off. There are times even today that I miss her kindness and warmth. She was the most selfless person I have ever known; she will be a part of me forever. On June 10, 1968 Patricia Carry Harrity Phillips was laid to rest. She had left this earth, but she will never leave my heart.

9

The Mommy Years

Saying good-bye to my mother was difficult and it was followed by even more difficult times in the life of a newly wed. Joe finished law school and passed the bar exam. Because he had been in Army ROTC as an undergraduate at Purdue, he had been in inactive reserves while in law school. Law school completed, it was time for him to fulfill his military commitment. This was 1968 and the height of the Vietnam conflict. Initially he was sent to Ft. Belvoir, VA for his officers training program. While he was there, I began my first semester of work on my Master's Degree. In the 1960's some schools would allow you to jump directly into the doctoral program, but most were still recommending the Master's Degree first. Since my goal was to eventually teach at the college level, I needed to get started on my graduate degrees. It was a difficult time to be apart, but we both knew that it was what was required of both of us. Since the officers' training was a non-dependent assignment, we were not allowed to see each other for most of it. About the time Joe finished his assignment, they allowed spouses to come and visit. I remember driving around VA to find a place to stay for the night. We had been apart so long, but now that we were together, we had to go hunting for a hotel–so much for advanced planning.

Joe's next assignment was in Ft. Leonard Woods, MO. This time I was able to join him, so I left Purdue at the end of fall semester and moved to a trailer in Devils Elbow, MO. We had one car, which Joe took to work each day. We also owned a radio that periodically could pick up a signal. The transition from the stimulation of a class one research university to a 'hollar' in the Ozarks was mind numbing. I tried to convince Joe to let me take him to work, but he wanted the car with him. I did finally land a regular substitution job, so Joe had to let me have the car. The good news was that we did make it on to base housing shortly thereafter. It was a good thing since I had read every book the little general store sold–twice, and was going bonkers in the silence.

Because this was the time of the Vietnam conflict, all of the officers were anxious as to what was going to happen to them. Many of the officers were electing to go "Vol indef", meaning they volunteered to stay in active duty for at least an additional year with the promise that they would be the last ones selected go to the front, most likely they would be sent to Korea. Joe was not cut out for the military and he did not want to extend his time any longer than necessary. I should add that I was not a very good military wife because I would not shun or avoid the enlisted men and women as well as their spouses. At that point in time, the military was very strict about that.

Our time in Ft. Leonard Wood passed and soon Joe's papers arrived. He was being sent to Seoul, Korea–headquarters. His was a non-dependent tour. Many of the officers there were able to house sit for embassy employees who were visiting stateside, but we did not have that opportunity. Joe's job was to approve any requests for new equipment, but because there was also a message being sent that the U.S. was pulling back on the base deployment, it meant that he had very little to do for his time in Korea.

While Joe was in Korea, I was back in Lafayette. We had purchased a tiny modular home and I returned to Purdue to finish my Master's degree. My assignment was to run the biology labs for the biology course for elementary education majors. It was exciting and a wonderful opportunity to learn. I loved being in Lilly Hall of Life Sciences. Dr. Michael Rossman, crystallographer renown for his identification of the structure of insulin, would set up his slide projector in the basement of Lilly and project images of cross sections of crystals on the far wall of the hallway. Hung on the wall was a large piece of white paper and he and his assistants would trace the image that was projected onto the paper. My how technology has advanced. Now they can do in days what took him years to do.

Not everything was pleasant in Lilly Hall of Life Science. In the days before sexual harassment, life could be very difficult for a woman alone in a man's world. As a scientist I was very much in the minority among graduate students. Thankfully there were a few other women, but the people with the power were all men. One man in particular decided I would be his sport. I had to check the area around our chemical storage rooms to be sure I was not going to be attacked when I went in to get some chemicals for a lab. Working late at night was also a danger. I never complained and I never reported what happened, but I also never forgot.

I finished all of my coursework for my Masters and the only thing remaining was to take a competency exam. This could be taken anywhere in the world as long as there was a proctor. I took Purdue at its word and took my exam in the BOQ (bachelor officers quarters) in Seoul, Korea. My proctor was a physician who also lived in the BOQ. In June of 1970 I flew from Indianapolis, Indiana to Tokyo, Japan where Joe met me for his R&R. We spent two weeks touring Japan and it was wonderful. The ancient cities of Nara and Kyoto were like an enchanted land–beautiful and filled with history and architectural wonders. From Japan we headed back to Korea and his BOQ.

The military is interesting; they had no objections to girlfriends living with the officers in the BOQ's, but they did not want wives living there. For the three and a half months that I stayed there, I played a game of cat and mouse with the MP's. We had a wonderful maid who really wanted to come state side so I taught her how to prepare American dishes and she in turn did two things for me. She was able to purchase vegetables in markets that she knew to be disease free, and she would warn me if I was in the room and the MP's were around. When the MP's were around I would lock the door. They would come into the hooch and demand that she open the door. In her sweet innocent way she would say, "no can do, Captain Speece change lock, no can do." I would lay low for a while and then she would give me the all-clear knock on the door.

The fall colors were just beginning to paint the trees when I returned to Indiana. Joe was to follow a few weeks later. It was difficult for him to decide what he wanted to do, but finally he was offered a job as the corporate counsel with a trucking firm in Muncie, Indiana. We sold the house in Lafayette and moved to Muncie. It did not take us long to find a lovely ranch home that would be perfect for a starting family. We just did not have the family started. Just before the beginning of the school year of 1971 I was offered a job at Wes Del High School in Gaston, Indiana. Joe was finally practicing law and I was ready to settle into my teaching. A few weeks after I signed the contract, I discovered I was finally pregnant and on May 15, 1972, Ryan Joseph Speece came into this world. At 9lb. 13 oz. and 21" he was not a small baby and he would never be average in size. He is now a strapping 6' 6" and airline pilot trim.

In 1972, women's rights had not quite made it to Gaston, Indiana. The school felt it was inappropriate for pregnant women to be in the classroom. They made me quit teaching two months before Ryan was born, they did, however, allow me to come back and teach in the fall. I was to stay with Wes Del until June of 1976. I had many wonderful students in the years at Wes Del, had my second child while sponsoring the senior class in 1974. Nicole Suzanne Speece almost did not make it to term as she thought that my climbing to the top of a 16' stepladder to hang decorations for a class dance was the time to enter the world. Bed rest for a week settled her down and we stayed connected for another five months. Since she was to be my second C-section, the doctor decided we needed a tax deduction so he scheduled her birth for December 31, 1974. The doctor was jealous when he took her out and discovered she had more hair than he did.

I continued teaching at Wes Del, but my goal had always been that I would get my doctorate and teach at the University level. Joe and I had talked about it even before we married. I took a few doctoral courses, but I wanted more. In

1976 I tendered my resignation at Wes Del and began my role as Doctoral Fellow at Ball State University. Luckily we had also moved into a wonderful, older, larger home right on the edge of the university campus the previous year. Nicole was 6 months old when we moved in and that would be the only home she would know until I moved to California in 1995.

The doctoral program was interesting, but I knew it was a means to an end. I wanted to teach at the college level, so I needed the doctorate. What I did not realize at the time was that an EdD would not help as much as a PhD, but the EdD was what was available, so I went for it. While working on my doctorate in Education, with a cognate in biology, I was able to finally get a part-time job teaching at Anderson College (it became a University several years after I joined the faculty.) In reflection, I did regret having not gotten a PhD over the years, but with my postdoctoral studies in 1994 in protein biochemistry, my legitimacy in the sciences was confirmed. I doubt that I would have gotten the job in California had I not had the EdD and I would not have gotten the job with Penn State University without having had the job in California, so all things have worked out for the best.

Two other events began to take shape around this time. I began to get more involved with the Hoosier Association of Science Teachers, Inc. (HASTI) and the National Science Teachers Association (NSTA) and I began to notice Joe's increased unhappiness with me. At the time I did not see the correlation, but in hindsight they could have been related. Actually it was not my involvement with HASTI that was the problem; it was the success I was having that was likely the problem. I moved from being a district director, to president of the organization, to a district director of the national organization and then the coordinator for both state and national conventions, to finally serving on the National Research Council's Chair's Advisory Board for the development of the *National Science Education Standards*.

Keeping a balance between children's needs, husband's needs, teaching demands and professional development needs was a difficult balance to maintain. I did all that I could to keep that balance, but life happens and we have to deal with it. My involvement with the national events became more and more problematic for Joe. He never said so directly, but when the activity that gives you great satisfaction is demeaned and belittled constantly, it takes its toll. Likewise, I was less able to deal with Joe's unhappiness (which would always miraculously disappear when I would finally get down).

There were good days in our marriage and two wonderful children were the product of the union, but when the pain out weighed the joys it was time to choose life. Finally, after 22 years together, we put the marriage to rest. Joe was and is a good man; we just had grown apart and no longer had a common goal.

10

The Pond and the Mulberry tree

916 Warwick Road was my dream home. Growing up, we would visit my aunts and uncle in Winnetka, Illinois. I loved the village and the home that Aunt Grace, Aunt Betty and Uncle Don had. (You can see their neighborhood and even their home or the one down the street that was its clone because it was used in the movie "Home Alone".) Aunt Grace and Aunt Betty were my father's sisters and Uncle Don was Grace's husband. They were the rich relatives. Uncle Don had owned a lumberyard for decades and had been very successful. Don was a short wiry man of very few words, but I always knew he was a kind and caring man. He loved to ride horses and had grown up thinking he would be a cowboy until he moved to the city. I understand that when he and Grace moved to Arizona in their retirement, he rode almost until the day he died. Any way, I loved Winnetka and the region of Muncie, known as Westwood where the university President's home and the home of the president of Ball Corp. were located—which reminded me of Winnetka.

For months, when I drove up and down Riverside Road, I had noticed a for sale sign down one road in the Westwood neighborhood. Finally I convinced Joe that we needed more space. The structural support for the home that we were in would not allow us to put a second story on the house and the water table was not conducive to building toward the back yard. If we wanted more space, we would have to move. Joe spoke with a realtor friend and we went to see the house. Now realtors will tell you that some folks have vision of possibilities and others do not. I guess I am one of those who is blessed with that vision. We walked into a home whose cedar shingles had been painted pink and whose interior was amazingly dirty. The house had been vacant for quite some time, the oil soot had never been cleaned out of the basement and people had tracked that oil soot on their shoes throughout the house. Additionally, paint was hanging from the ceiling. This is not exactly the condition one would expect in that neighborhood, but it meant that two "fixer-uppers" could afford the home. I knew just how the house could look. There was wonderful charm and warmth that was just begging to be teased from the filth and neglect. The sun could stream into the large windows in the dining room and living room and I knew this was the right place to be. A low bid, some negotiations and soon we were the owners of a new home. Thankfully we did not have much difficulty selling our old home and in May of 1975 we began working on some immediate renovations before moving into our new home.

Several years after moving into the home, one of my next-door neighbors asked if I had found the pond in the back yard. I had no idea what he was talking about, but he explained that one of the early owners had constructed a semi-circular pond that had a 14' diameter and a depth of almost 4'. The winter after it was constructed, a neighbor's little boy came over to play at the pond. Thinking it was frozen; he stepped onto the ice and quickly fell through. Luckily a college student walking behind the house saw this and pulled the little boy out. Mortified, the homeowners filled their lovely pond with dirt and stones and never saw it again.

Being a good inquisitive scientist, I just had to go hunting; I knew that there appeared to be a piece of buried concrete in one region of the back yard. Thinking that could be part of the lip of the pond, I took a garden spade and began to tease away the dirt. As though I was on an archeological dig, I inched my way around this structure. Ryan was curious as well, so one summer day we decided to really get serious at digging out this pond. Even at six years old, Ryan was a very strong child. Having his help was almost like having an adult there with me. We found bones that might have been the remains of someone's pet dog, some bottles and flagstone. I suspect that they had landscaped the pond with the stones and when they filled it, they just dumped the flagstones into the pond. Some of the stones were very heavy even for me, but Ryan thought he was Superman and actually hefted some very significant stones out of the pond.

What was amazing was the fact that the marine paint that they had used—perhaps as much as 35 years previously was still there. That was both good and bad. It was good in that it had preserved the concrete, but bad because it created a very slick surface. As our afternoon progressed I needed to go in and begin fixing dinner. I cautioned Ryan not to take any heavy stones out, but to just work on the dirt in the pond. I had been in the house perhaps 10 minutes when I heard him crying. Ryan was a typical baby and would cry when hungry, wet, or tired, but he did not cry as a child. He might get hurt, but he just did not cry much. For him to come in and be crying meant that something was seriously wrong! As it turned out, he had tried to lug a 70 lb. stone out of the pond. He slipped on the surface and ended up dropping the stone and trapping his left thumb and index finger under the stone. I suspected that he had broken the bones, so I tucked Nicole and Ryan into the car, called Joe and told him to meet me at the hospital. The emergency room doctor was unimpressed since there were no cuts, just scrapes. He was just about to leave the room when I indicated that this was a child who did not cry, for him to still be crying, although he was trying not to, meant that something was amiss. The doctor finally agreed to X-ray and of course there were two broken metacarpal bones.

In spite of Ryan's injury, we did proceed to unearth the pond. We were totally surprised by the sheer size of the pond, the steepness of the slope of the sides and the wonderful potential for landscaping. We created an upper pond and a waterfall going into the big pond. Years later I would meet a person who had attended some conference at Ball State University and I indicated that they probably knew where I lived. Of course they knew that they could not possibly know where I lived, until I said "white picket fence and pond with waterfall." The lights would go on and they remembered the lovely backyard.

Our back yard bordered on the parking lot for the Teachers College building and the Industrial Arts building. In the summertime there was a photography course that was taught in the IA building. I am sure that the professors who taught that course had a whole collection of photos chronicling the growth of my children. Invariably I would look out the kitchen window to see what Ryan and Nicole were up to and see some student with a camera poking through the picket fence, trained on my two children.

Amazingly enough we never had any serious vandalism by students. Occasionally we would have a student taking a shortcut through the yard and we even had one very gutsy student who would park in my driveway and walk to class. That did not last long as I came home from school early one day and just waited for the student. We did, however have one rather humorous visit by two students. Our dog Bandit was a very friendly dog, but one night she got me up and wanted to go outside. I padded downstairs and let her out the back door. She headed towards the back yard and stopped. She dropped her tail and began to growl. This was highly uncharacteristic for her so I walked outside to try and see what she was looking at beyond the garage. Just as I got to the corner of the garage I saw a young man and woman who had been seated on the edge of my pond. By the time I could see them, he had jumped up and was zipping up his jeans. As soon as he was together, he ran away leaving the young woman to fend for herself. I gently said to the young woman, "just remember how he protected you." She apologized for being there and left. Bandit had it right, once the boy left, she was happy and went to eagerly greet the young woman. I wonder if that young woman ever thinks of her interlude in our back yard.

Although it was a fairly small back yard, the trees were all mature and offered a delightful haven for the children as they grew or for all of us if we wanted to have a picnic in the back yard. One of the trees that arose at the back edge of the property and around which we had to construct our picket fence was a mulberry tree. Just as I had done as a child, my children would climb the mulberry tree to watch students walking to and from classes. Each summer I would go out and pick mulberries and make a savory mulberry-cinnamon preserve. There was no way that I could pick all the mulberries and many would fall to the ground or onto the ledge of the picket fence. Being a biologist, I believed in letting nature recycle, so I did not rake up the fallen mulberries. Nature being what it is, in the process of recycling the mulberries would ferment. Did you know that blue jays and squirrels can get drunk? It was the funniest thing to watch the blue jays after they had consumed too many of the fermented berries. They would sit on the fence and squawk as loud as they could and then fall off the fence. Squirrels faired no better. They were the common fox squirrels and after too many berries, thought they had evolved into flying squirrels. They would climb to the top of the tall oak tree behind the pond and think that they could fly over to the mulberry tree. In the inebriated state they often misjudged the distance. Typically they ended up in the pond, soaked, but alive. Because the garage had a flat deck, the kids and I could go out onto the roof and watch the "fermentation circus."

While it was funny to watch, it served as an excellent lesson for the children. Too much alcohol causes people and animals to do stupid things. When Ryan decided to become a pilot, he personally selected to never drink because he did not want to risk his career. Likewise, Nicole always serves as the designated driver for many of her friends. If she does want to have something to drink it is always in moderation. Powerful early lessons!

11

Anderson University

I was in the second year of my doctoral program at Ball State and wanted to try and find a teaching job to supplement my doctoral fellowship. I knew there was a private, church related college in Anderson, IN, so I made an appointment to meet with the Provost. Dr. Robert Nicholson, who would later become the president of the college. He was most gracious and we had an interesting conversation. While I was hoping for a bit more, I did end up teaching a health class for them in that first year with Anderson. I did well in that class, graduated from Ball State and was given a few more classes to teach. Finally in 1980 I became a full time faculty member of the biology department.

I was very fortunate to have a string of wonderful students at Anderson University, some of whom I still maintain contact. One student who became like a surrogate son has brought me great pleasure as an educator. Early in his career I could see leadership potential, but there was also a great deal of insecurity. Much of what you get to do when you teach at a small university is to help the young folks make it safely to adulthood. I always knew when Wayne was struggling with personal issues, so I would invite him to come to the office to get it off his shoulders. At one point he had a girlfriend whom he thought he would marry. They had even purchased some furniture together. The problem was that she did not value his educational experience and did not understand why he would not quit school so they could get on with their life. I could not tell him what to do, but I could ask questions that helped him crystallize what he valued and what he needed to feel successful in life. Thankfully he figured out what he wanted and what he did not want and ended the relationship.

Wayne was a lab assistant for me for several years and I knew what he was capable of doing. When it came time to apply to graduate school, he decided that he wanted to go to Purdue in the School of Entomology. Purdue only had so many fellowships and it was down to Wayne and a student from some other school. The folks at Purdue were not familiar with Anderson University and the rigor of our academic program. Since I was an alumna of Purdue and knew a few folks in Entomology, I placed a call to the person who had written to Wayne. I convinced them that I was familiar with Purdue's standards and I had absolutely no doubt that he was up to the challenge. We might not have an entomology program, but I felt that Wayne could compete. A few weeks later we got the word, he was in!! Once we had him in the door, Purdue's door for Anderson University students was wide open, he set the bar high. Wayne is now teaching and doing wonderful things at the University of North Carolina.

I mentioned that Anderson University was a church related school, it is most definitely. It is conservative, though not on the level of a Bob Jones University. There is little tolerance in the church or school for behavior out of their described norms. Two situations brought that home quite forcefully. I would always go to a colleague's class on human sexuality (taught in the sociology department) and teach the section on the biology of human reproduction. One time I got off on a tangent about testosterone and how it was used as a performance enhancer, but not without side effects. When the class ended, an older student asked if he could walk me to my office. I said of course and we began to discuss further the effects of testosterone. When we got to my office I could tell that he was troubled about something and I asked if he wanted to talk more. He said yes. We went up to my office and he began to tell me a story that curled my toes. He also said that I was the only one he could trust with the story. He had been part of a Delta seek and destroy team in Vietnam. The team was given testosterone to make them more aggressive, uppers to rev them up and downers to bring them down after a successful mission. The specifics of what he shared with me would be inappropriate to discuss here, but what is relevant was the fact that he knew that had he told anyone else at the college what he told me, there would be extreme judgment. That was not what he needed; he needed help in dealing with his issue. Over the next two months we met regularly and I believe that he was successful in dealing with those issues, and his thank you letter, received several years after the event confirmed that we did the right thing.

Another sequence of events took place over several years. In 1985 I began to work with the CDC and some primary researchers to try and understand this new disease, AIDS that was affecting so many young homosexual men. I was troubled by the treatment homosexuals were receiving and I was mortified by the statement some folks around the country were making that AIDS was God's way of punishing them. As I struggled with how I could help, I knew that education was the key to reducing prejudice. My daughter was reading Charlotte Bronte's *Jane Eyre*. She came to me one evening and said "I have the perfect quote for you Mom, you can use it with your AIDS presentations." She was absolutely correct. The quote, which is still at the end of all of my e-mails is, "Prejudices, it is well known, are most difficult to eradicate from the heart whose soil has never been loosened or fertilized by education; they grow there firm as weeds among stones." There were several gay students who, by word of mouth, found out that I was a safe haven for them. Anderson had pretty much of the military's attitude, "don't ask and don't tell." Yet these young folks needed to know that they were valued members of the community and they were still loved by God. I know I am, even today, going to raise some objections when I say this, but my God is a loving god and He created all of us. For the most part, homosexuality is a genetic condition, how can we say it is wrong.

Eventually I was asked by a group of adult members of the church who also were members of PFLAG (Parents and Friends of Lesbians and Gays) if I would come and talk to them about HIV/AIDS and later about the genetics of sexual orientation. I was happy to do this and hoped that I was giving these parents and friends some concrete education so that they could understand their loved ones. One summer the group invited Mel White to come and conduct a daylong workshop. I was asked to come and meet Mel, which I was happy to do. Mel got into his presentation and then stopped. He indicated that they all needed to know more about the genetics of sexual orientation and asked me to come up and provide some information. This was unexpected, but again, I was happy to do so. Now this workshop was taking place at the same time that a weeklong camp meeting was taking place. We are not talking about a few folks pitching tents; the population of Anderson grows by about 10,000 during this camp meeting. Our little sequestered group was definitely on the fringe.

We were so much on the fringe that the next morning when I went to my office to grab some papers before flying to Washington DC for a meeting with the National Research Council (a branch of the National Academy of Science) I discovered someone had broken into my office. That is not exactly correct, they had entered with a key because there was no forced entry. Our building had just undergone some major renovations and the new locks had just been installed two days before. Very few people had any of the new keys. What had been done in my office was all symbolic, but it was clearly an attempt to try and stop me from talking about homosexuality. I knew we would never discover who had entered my office, but what they did not understand was that that just fueled me.

Several of the gay students learned of the break-in and they were initially worried about whether they could still come and talk with me. It did not take them long to discover that I was still there to listen to them and to help them mentally work through whatever it was that was on their minds.

I still recall one annual evaluation session I had. I knew that my students, a significant percentage of whom were going on to medical school or graduate school, were doing well on their MCAT's and GRE's. This said to me that they were getting the kind of education they needed in my classes, as well as that of my colleagues. I was not concerned about my ability to teach the science, but I really wanted to be sure that I was being a good role model for the students. During the annual review, I mentioned that my goal was to be known as the compassionate professor to whom the students could come. My evaluator was not happy with that. He thought I should want to be known as the best scientist. I did not want to insult him, but I already knew from the students that they already felt that way. As the only woman in any of the sciences I really felt he was holding me to a different standard than my male counterparts.

I met with considerable resistance and skepticism when I made a major change in my cell biology class. I really wanted the students to understand what it meant to conduct true research. Rather than use a "cook-book" approach to the labs, the students devised experiments that would help them more fully understand the concepts we were studying. It was difficult at first, because they had to learn how to ask the right questions, but once they got the hang of it, they really became proficient in designing experiments. Years later I would hear, time and again from former students that they really learned how to be a scientist in that cell biology class.

It was most gratifying when a few years ago a group of new Penn State faculty members came to visit our campus and among the group was a young biochemist who had been one of my students at Anderson University. It was humbling to have her tell me that it was I who had influenced her and sustainer her when she was having doubts about her career choices. Only weeks ago I received a phone call from another student who works for a scientific supply corporation (after spending many years teaching) and he was calling me for my professional opinion on an educational matter. Life does go in wonderful circles, and yes, I do believe that I was able to have a positive impact on the lives of many of my students.

My colleagues at Anderson University were an interesting lot. As I indicated earlier, my father just did not know how to support me in what I did, but there was one exception. When I became the chair of the biology department at Anderson University he sent me a planter. It was the only time in my life that I can recall his ever indicating he was proud of me. That planter/terrarium was nurtured and pampered to keep it alive in my office. There were no windows, so it did not get any natural light and it was a challenge to keep things alive. One December it was looking pretty sad, so I put some new plants in it and set it out in the hallway on one of the tables where we had much of the department's plant collection. There were south facing windows, so we had a mini-greenhouse. The hallway was protected during vacations and at night by some security gates at each end. When I came back after Christmas vacation my planter/terrarium was gone. I was angry and devastated. The only acknowledgement my father had ever offered had been stolen. Imagine my surprise when one of my colleagues invited Joe and me to come and play bridge at their home several weeks later and I saw my planter on their piano. I asked the wife about the planter and she gushed that she just loved the Christmas present her husband had given to her. I did not have the heart to tell her; after all, we all knew that he tended towards kleptomania.

12

A Trip to the Dunes

While at Anderson University I would teach a summer section of Human Ecology. The most significant field trip we would take would be a trip to the Indiana Dunes National Lake Shore. Located on the southeast edge of Lake Michigan, the Dunes have, for more than a century represented the best place in the world to study ecological succession. Since the area of study is only about a four-hour drive from campus, it made for a delightful one day outing for the class. Normally I could get everyone into a 15-passenger van, though some times one or two carloads of students would follow as well.

One year our trip was to be more memorable than anticipated. The date selected to go up to the dunes turned out to have some conflicts for some of the students, but they wanted to experience as much of the trip as possible. As a result, we had two carloads of students as well as one of the school's 15 passenger vans. There was some extra room in the van, so on this trip I took my two children with me. I went to pick up the van early the morning of the trip and was not pleased to find that it had not been cleaned out after the last usage. I did a quick walk through with the kids help (they were about 10 and 13 at the time.)

Everyone reconnoitered at the designated spot and we were on the road by 7:00 a.m. On the way up to the dunes I would do a little travel-log for the students. We talked about the different soil types we were seeing and the different climax communities that would likely be found in the areas we were driving through. When you are talking about ecological succession, the first plants and animals to inhabit a barren land are called the pioneer community. The pioneer community gradually gives way to more complex organisms until you reach the final stable community known as the climax community. For more than a century it was thought that the climax community was the end, but research data from the past 10-15 years has put some doubt on that theory.

The closer we got to Valparaiso, IN the more erratic the van seemed to be driving. Since it had two gasoline tanks, I flipped the switch to the other tank. That seemed to improve things for a short while. As we were driving through Valparaiso, the van began to chug as if it were out of gasoline, I pulled to the side of the road and thankfully one of the carloads of students pulled in behind me. There were some jokes about woman driver and not checking the gasoline. Since both tanks were relatively full, I knew that was not the problem, but I also knew that gasoline was not getting to the engine. My guess was a bad fuel pump, but being almost 150 miles from campus, that was not a good thing. The students in the car went and got some gasoline. We put some in the tank, but I remembered reading somewhere that you needed to put some gasoline in the carburetor in order to get a vehicle going again. The van we were driving was an older Dodge van and the carburetor was under a carpeted area between the passenger and driver's seat. I removed the covering and the top of the carburetor, poured a little gasoline into the well and the van started right up. I put everything back together and we were on the road again. Just before we made it to the parking lot of the Dunes, the van died again so I repeated the process and we made it to our destination. I was most concerned about the van, but hoped that by having the day to cool down, we would be able to make it back to the University.

The day at the Dunes was great. The weather was perfect and there was much to see. Normally I try to lead the group, making it to each rise of a dune ahead of the students. The dunes are notorious for youthful trysts and rather than embarrass my students or the young lovebirds, I try to give everyone a chance. This year was one of those years where that practice came in handy. As I crested the rise of one dune, I saw two young folks totally engrossed in each other. I stopped my students and in a rather loud voice directed them to observe some unique aspect of succession behind them. The lovebirds finally heard me and made a hasty exit. The coast cleared, we proceeded with our walk. Of course the college students caught on very quickly and had some fun with that fact.

One of the things that I talk about while at the dunes is the fact that the dunes are constantly moving, sometimes at a rate of 30' per year. One of my students, a talented cartoonist picked up on this concepts and gave me a drawing that shows me looking ahead and saying "Now the interesting thing about these sand dunes is that they migrate at their own pace despite the efforts of humanity to control them...Does anybody know why that is?...." The other bubble indicating that I am thinking says "I hate that awkward silence after I ask a question...." Behind me is a huge sand dune that has obviously suddenly moved and has trapped all the students in the hill. No wonder they did not answer. Needless to say, we had fun on the trips.

Because Ryan and Nicole were on the trip with me I had a chance to show off how much they had learned and they loved being in the spotlight. Often they would answer one of my questions before the students even realized that a question had been asked. They were learning at a young age how to fit into college classes–something that would serve them well several years later as they both took college courses while they were still in high school.

After a wonderful day at the Dunes, it was time to head back to Anderson. We made it just past one gasoline station when the van went out again. I repeated the procedure that I had used before and nothing happened. I put yet a little more gasoline into the carburetor and then something happened, but certainly not what I wanted, there was a fire in the carburetor. I yelled at everyone to get out of the van and to be sure they got my kids out. The only thing I had to put out the fire was my new jacket. Without a second thought, I grabbed the jacket and smothered the fire. Clearly we were not going anywhere soon. We walked down to the gas station but they did not have a service person. They called another station in town and they brought out a tow truck. I was the only person allowed to ride in the tow truck, so I gave the students some money and sent them to the Pizza Hut along with my children to spend the rest of the afternoon.

At the service station they finally agreed with me that the fuel pump was out. It took them quite a while to locate one, but they finally got it and installed the pump. As I waited, the young man who was manning the service station decided that I would be his "mother confessor." I learned far more about his love life that I ever wanted to know. I suppose he pegged me as the "motherly" type and hoped I would be a good listener. Finally I was on my way, but as I headed back to pick up everyone, the van died at an intersection. This time it acted more like a dead battery. I was next to another service station and they jump started me, so I was off again.

Given the behavior of the van, I was afraid to stop it. Luckily when I got back to the Pizza Hut Ryan and Nicole were sitting outside waiting. I had them get everyone else and we were finally on the road. By now it was about 9 or 9:30 p.m.

A little before 10 we were near Plymouth, IN and I could tell that my lights were getting dimmer and dimmer. I could not believe that I not only was sent out in a van with a bad fuel pump, but one with a bad battery as well. One mile from the exit the van just stopped. I was able to get it to the side of the road and some of the young men agreed to walk to the exit ahead where there was a gas station. They arrived just as the folks were getting ready to lock up, but they were good Samaritans and came and got the van with their tow truck. There was no way they could take care of the van that evening and there was no one answering at Anderson University. The one young station attendant said that his father-in-law owned a Rent-a-Wreck. I thought I already had a wreck, but asked it there might be a full sized station wagon that I could squeeze everyone into. He got his father-in-law out of bed, but he was another kind soul and soon we had an old, but very large station wagon. Everyone piled in, including my two back in the very back. Around 2:00 a.m. we made it back to the University, and everyone was exhausted. I told the students in the car that they did not have to come in to take their exam later that morning; they could take it on Monday.

Since there were other students who did not get tied up in our Dunes trip from Hell, I knew they would be there bright and early to take their exam. That meant I had to be there as well. I not only got there, but I got there early enough to go see the Provost. I had complained about the lack of maintenance on the fleet vehicles before, but no one seemed interested in taking my concerns seriously. To add to that, the folks at the motor pool expected me to take the station wagon back up to Plymouth. I told them that it was their fault and they needed to take it back and get the van that I left up there. When I spoke with the Provost he agreed and called them to tell them what they were going to do. He also paid to replace my new jacket.

I am quite sure that none of the students who went on that dunes trip will ever forget the day.

13

Life Begins After 40

In the 1980's or there about, there was a book that came out entitled *Life Begins at Forty*. I was just a few years behind, but at age 42 I went whitewater rafting for the first time, true primitive camping for the first time, and began learning how to snow ski. At age 49 I became SCUBA certified and went on my first of many warm water dives around the world. My marriage was in serious decline, but I had finally decided not to go down with it. Though the marriage would languish for another two years I had decided that I was not going to give up on life.

A colleague from one of the national professional societies I belonged to, Dr. Ivo Lindauer, talked me into going on his Ecology and Geology of the Grand Canyon course field trip. The trip was a six-day, five night rafting trip through 183 miles of the Grand Canyon. Before the trip I had never rafted before and the only camping had been one night tent camping in very benign settings. I had no idea what to expect from the experience.

My anxieties were manifest in a dream that I had a few nights before leaving for my first rafting trip. In my dream we had stopped at a sandy point in the Canyon and had decided to take a swim to cool off. Being an old lifeguard, I was going to play that role. Before we could go swimming, in my dream, we needed to change into our bathing suits. I was to take the women into a cave to modestly change into our suits. Being a leader, I volunteered to go in first to be sure things were safe. I was confronted with a terrible smell. As I explored the cave, I came across a dead body. I would not let the women into the cave, but since it was a dream, they were instantly in their bathing suits, so it was not necessary. We called for a helicopter and they came and got the body. The dream jumped to the point where folks were swimming and I was sitting on the sand watching them. I suddenly realized that there were two rattlesnakes around me, one by my left foot and one next to my right hand. I knew that I needed to stay calm, so I was having this conversation with the snakes trying to explain to them that I ate foods with preservatives and it would not be healthy for them to try and eat me. My colleague in the water saw what was happening and began yelling for me to not move. The yelling startled the snakes and they began to chomp on me (yes, I know that is not how snakes eat—but this was my dream.) I guess you could say that I had a few anxieties going into the trip.

Getting to my first rafting trip—there were 10 total—was a page out of the "Perils of Pauline." I was scheduled to fly from Indianapolis to Denver, meet a van from the University of Northern Colorado at the airport Holiday Inn at I-70 and I-25 at 9:00 a.m. I was up around 3:00 a.m. in order to make the hour and a half drive to Indianapolis to catch my 6:00 a.m. flight. I arrived at the Denver airport and got into a cab and asked them to take me to the airport Holiday Inn. I settled into the lobby to wait for the van. Nine came and went, ten came and went and I started to get a bit concerned. I placed a few calls to the University of Northern Colorado, but no one knew anything. Finally I had this uneasy feeling that maybe I was not in the right place. I went to the desk and asked if I was in deed at the airport Holiday Inn at I-70 and I-25. They said they were the airport Holiday Inn, but they were only at I-70. There was another Holiday Inn several miles down I-70 at the intersection with I-25. We called there and were told there had been some folks waiting around, but they were no longer there.

Since the group was going to camp overnight at Arches National Park, I thought I could rent a car and try to catch up with them. Once I found out the cost of the car rental for a week (in the days of no free mileage) it was out of the question. I checked to see what it would cost to fly to Page, AZ and that was within the realm of possibilities. The hitch was that I had to be back at the airport in 20 minutes. Amazingly enough I made it in time. In time to sit in the plane for more than 50 minutes while some fix was attended. Finally we were airborne and I was on my way to a new adventure. We changed planes in Las Vegas, and St. George, UT and finally landed in the tiny Page, AZ airport. Since we had been in a very small plane, it did not take long to get the luggage. I had a large suitcase with both rafting clothes and clothes I would need to do a consulting job at the University of Northern Colorado after the rafting trip. I was also carrying a "boat bag" that had my sleeping bag a few clothes and the bottle of wine the stewardess had given to me before we landed in Las Vegas. I took the boat bag as carry-on luggage and the larger suitcase was in the hold. That is, it was supposed to be in the hold, but no luggage for me came off the plane.

Still operating under a degree of naivety, I figured I could rent a car or get a cab to take me to Marble Canyon Lodge at Lee's Ferry where I could join the first rafting group that would be getting off the river that day. Silly me. There were no car rentals, cabs, public conveyance or any other way to get to Marble Canyon Lodge EXCEPT, to either rent a plane or take a 1/2-day rafting trip there. I called Marble Canyon Lodge and asked to be connected to my friend's room. It turns out that there were no phones in the rooms, so that was not possible. I left a message and hoped that it would get to him, there were some doubts since I had to spell almost every word. My luck had finally turned and an hour later, the pay phone in the airport rang and it was my friend. There was someone there who had come to visit and they were coming to Page to do laundry so they would come to pick me up. By the time we all got back to the Lodge and finally called it a day, I had been up for 24 hours. You would think I would have instantly fallen asleep, but it would be a few more nights before I actually slept.

The next day the van arrived and everyone piled out and started asking Ivo if he knew anything about the person they were supposed to pick up in Denver. We all had a good laugh about it and began our preparations to begin our trip the next day.

For the rafting trips through the Canyon we used 36' military pontoon boats with 25 horsepower motors. There were two baloney tubes on the sides with the baggage in the middle. Each of the boats could hold up to 18 people and several tons of baggage. Every night we would sleep on cots under the stars. Every day we would hike the side canyons to explore the geology and ecology of the canyon. Each participant was expected to give a presentation on some aspect of the Canyon during the trip. Tour West was the outfitter that we used and over the ten trips, I always asked that Terry Johnson be our head boatman. He was a mountain of a man with a heart of gold. He knew the Canyon and more importantly, he knew the Colorado River. With Terry, safety and fun were partners. During the school year Terry was an elementary school principal and I am sure that his children loved him.

My first trip down the Colorado River was a life changing experience. I was physically challenged to do things I never thought I could do and personally I was forced to let go of some inhibitions. There is no privacy in the canyon. There were no caves to change clothes in (as in my dreams) and there is precious little vegetation to change behind. Bathing in the river took place only at the river's edge since the water moved too swiftly to actually get out into the river to submerge. Those sponge baths were very quick as well since the water temperature ranged between 47° and 57 ° F. This means if you really wanted to get clean, someone was going to be observing. True, we had the men go downstream and the women upstream, but modesty pretty much went out the window. As I made subsequent trips, I promised every participant that they would come out with a new perspective of themselves and of life. There is an awesome power and beauty in the Canyon that seeps into every fiber of one's being.

I partially solved some of the privacy issues by being the first one up and dressed each morning. I would rise with the first rays of sunlight, usually a little before 5:00 a.m. and go down to the river to bathe. Normally no one else was moving at that time, but on one of the trips Verdy Pedicord was as much of an early riser as I had been. One morning she climbed over the rocks to our little bathing area and found that I was already there. She said that I reminded her of Paul Chabas's painting *September Morn*. I was unfamiliar with the painting by name and a few months after our trip, she sent a print to me, which I now have framed, and hanging in my bathroom.

Because I made so many excellent friends from Colorado while rafting the Grand Canyon, I was encouraged to consider skiing. Since I was doing some consulting with UNC, I was able to go out to Colorado in the wintertime. While I have only been on the Colorado slopes periodically, I love the feeling of sliding down a mountainside. It is so exhilarating! I was able to take both of my children skiing with me at various times and now Nicole, a resident of Denver, has really gotten into skiing.

In 1994 I decided to take my first and only sabbatical. The purpose of the sabbatical was to put together a video that would vicariously take my ecology students to a variety of ecosystems. I planned to film the alpine ecosystem in the Rockies, the desert in the Great Basin Desert of Utah, the temperate rain forest of the Olympic Peninsula of Washington, the grasslands of Kansas, the deciduous forests of the Midwest and the tropical rain forests and marine ecosystems of Belize. Many, many miles later and many types of videotape later, I had had an exciting exploration of this continent. The trip to Belize was unlike anything I had experienced previously. The irony was the I almost did not get approval for my sabbatical. Sabbaticals to just vacation were easily approved, but one to actually gather data about world ecosystems was not taken seriously. Thankfully I was granted permission to take the sabbatical.

The first leg of my trip to Belize was to Ambergris Caye. What a beautiful little island. I stayed at the Caribbean Villa that was owned by Wil and Susan Lala. The Villa offered bicycles for their guests to use to get between the end of the island and the little village. When I arrived the last of the season's hurricanes had just come through and had ravaged the roads. Potholes were knee deep and significant enough in which to lose most of a bicycle. On my second day there, I had my 35 mm camera and video camera in the basket of the bicycle and decided to head into town. Negotiating the potholes was difficult at best, but I made it into town and had purchased the items I wanted at a little shop. I was on my route back to the Villa when I had an accident. The narrow ledge that I was trying to keep my bicycle on in order to miss the potholes just was not wide enough and soon I was falling into a water filled pothole. My first concern was for my cameras. I grabbed them and kept them in the air, but then I had no way to break my fall except with my leg and knee. There were no broken bones, but I had effectively filleted off the front of my leg. The remainder of the trek back to the Villa seemed to take forever. I was bleeding and in pain, but no one seemed to be concerned. When I finally made it to the Villa, Wil and Susan had left to go stateside and the replacement folks had not yet arrived. The person at the front desk did not know if they had any first aid equipment. I knew I needed an antibiotic and some gauze. The only thing I could do was to return to the village and the little store with a pharmacy. I purchased my supplies and sat outside the store and tended to my injuries.

Injuries aside, I was not about to delay my SCUBA dives. The salt water in my wounds was not great, but I did not even think about the fact that the wound might ooze blood and attract sharks. Thankfully nothing like that happened. The dives were enchanting and unlike anything I had ever experienced. I could have stayed down for hours, but of course that is not allowed. When the opportunity arises, I will go back to Belize and the Caribbean Villa on Ambergris Caye.

My time in paradise came to an end and I headed for the interior of Belize to the tropical jungle. Because the high season was not to begin for another week, I ended up being the only visitor at a five star spa. The food was great, the furniture in the rooms was beautifully crafted of mahogany sticks and dozens of fresh hibiscus flowers were placed around the room each day.

On the day that I planned to film in the jungle I got up with the sun and headed down the path that lead into the jungle. I was aware that this was an active jungle with anaconda, jaguars and all sorts of wild animals. While I did venture into the jungle from the path, I was always within sight of the path. I was able to capture the images I wanted and headed back to my room to get ready for breakfast and a trip to the Mayan ruins. Once in the room there was a knock on my door. They were concerned that they had not seen me up and about that morning. I told the young man where I had been and he was mortified. What he was able to explain to me was not a concern for the animals, but the cult group that lived in the jungle who had a preference for blond women. Actually, I read a report recently that indicated that Belize had been one of the major traffickers in humans until they cracked down on the piracy in the last few years. I was glad that I was out early; maybe they were all still sleeping in. Dodged that bullet.

14

The Grand Canyon

Though my post-doctoral research was in the area of protein biochemistry, my fascination has always been with the macrobiotic, specifically nature. From the early explorations in the Wisconsin woods to the underwater dives–nature continues to grab my mind and soul. No other nature-inspired experience had ever grabbed me as much as my trips through the Grand Canyon. Although I have spoken of the Grand Canyon trips, there were 10 total, there were so many wonderful experiences over the years that it warrants its own chapter.

There are a few different theories about the formation of the Grand Canyon, but from my vantage point on the Colorado River, I believe the idea that there was a combination of uplifting of land masses and the down cutting of the river to create this mile deep furrow in the ground. The trips we took through the Grand Canyon were part of a Geology and Ecology of the Grand Canyon course that was alternately taught through the University of Northern Colorado and Anderson University. We would spend several weekends before the trip in classroom settings studying the ancient inhabitants, art, geology and ecology of the canyon. We also spent considerable time talking about what to expect while in the Canyon and what to bring for the trip. We would all reconnoiter at Lees Ferry the night before the float trip began. The following account is taken from my journal on one of our trips, all events did in deed happen.

Lees Ferry:

The campground is set on a rise above the river. The deep red rocks of the Dakota sandstone are constantly being eroded by the wind and the fine stone particles act as sand blasters to every surface that is exposed. The group had shared a dinner at the Marble Canyon Lodge and now in the dark we are setting up our cots and campsites. The wind is relentless and some folks turn over picnic tables to serve as blinds against the wind and the blowing sand. That is what some folks did, but I wanted to take it all in. The sky was so clear that I could see millions and millions of stars. In my first night I saw more meteorites (shooting stars) than I had seen collectively in my entire life. Every few seconds there was another one. Being more than fifty miles from the nearest city, albeit a small one, there was no ambient light to interfere with the clear view of the sky. What a spectacle, forget any sleep that night.

Day One

It is a major undertaking to launch boats onto the Colorado River. Lees Ferry is 15 miles downstream from Glenn Canyon Dam and is one of the few places where the river and the land are at the same level. The National Parks system only allows 15,000 people to raft the Colorado River in the Grand Canyon each year, so the precise timing and regulation of launches helps to spread out the folks and thus enhance the experience for everyone.

After a sleepless night at the campground we make our way to the river. Each rafter had one boat-bag in which we had our sleeping bag and clothes, and one-day bag that was hopefully relatively waterproof where we kept things like sun-screen, trail mix and perhaps a long sleeved shirt to protect us from the sun. We could also carry a waterproof camera bag, but that was the extent of our baggage for the next six days. Each boat also carried cots and enough food and drink to last the entire time. Food is packed in ice and used in the order of likely thaw.

It is necessary for each boat company or individual rafter to leave no residuals behind. There are trash bags stored on the boat to be discarded once off the river and there are human waste bags that are likewise discarded after the trip.

The level of anticipation is extremely high as we wait for our opportunity to get underway. There is no shade, but while we wait we take our rafters on a little hike to the site of Lee's campsite. On the way we introduce the rafters to rabbit bush, sagebrush and the variety of lizards that are found in this region of the Canyon. Our rafters are quickly learning how important it is to hydrate and when we return to the staging area, we make sure that everyone has something to drink.

Soon we are finally on the river and beginning an adventure of a lifetime. On our left we can see the remains of the old trail that lead to the river where folks would take the ferry across. There is immediately a bend in the river and as we round the bend we can see the Navajo Bridge, which now serves the same function as the ferry did a century ago.

Through our six days and five nights we will encounter roughly 90 rapids in the 183 miles of river. Some will be small riffles, while one will be the fastest navigable white water in the northern hemisphere. We start our first encounter with rapids with the Pirea riffle. It is a baby rapid, but we are all so pumped, we yell as if we are on a monster roller coaster. This is going to be a good trip.

We have a relatively short day on the river this first day. We camp at South Canyon where we are able to explore Vasey's Paradise. This is a riparian haven. Fresh, clear water pours out of the rocks and lush vegetation grows wherever there is water. We take some of the boat's water reservoirs and fill them with the fresh water from Vasey's. There is also a gated cave up in the wall above the campsite. This is where Sutton stored some of his belongings before hiking out of the canyon as he abandoned his first attempt through the Canyon.

We take the rafters on a hike up a plateau where we are able to share with them pictographs and remains from an early Anasazi camp ground. For many of the rafters this is an entirely new ecosystem. The rocks, the vegetation are totally alien to anything they have previously encountered, but they are mesmerized.

Back down on the river level, we each set up our campsites. Boat bags are heavy and cots are awkward. The farther your campsite is from the boat, the more difficult it is to trudge through the loose sand. Even so, there is one spot that I always choose for my campsite. It is nested in some Tamarix and against a wall of Supai Group limestone. My campsite was set up and I grabbed a hand full of trail mix from the baggie in my day bag before heading back to the boats to help cook dinner. As I walk back to the main area the song of the Canyon Wren can be heard over the roar of the river. In fact there are very few places that you cannot hear the wren. The song is sweet, yet piercing. Once you have heard it, you will never forget it.

Meals in the Canyon, when you travel with Tour West are outstanding. There is always a tasty chicken stew, steaks, pork chops, Mexican fiesta, and at least on fish night. Breakfasts range from blueberry pancakes, to made-to-order omelets, egg sandwiches, French toast and scrumptious coffeecakes.

When I went back to my campsite I caught a glimpse of a ringtail cat that was trying to steal my bag of trail mix. Luckily I caught him just in time. That night I also was awaken by the sound of something on the rocks above my head. I looked up and there was the silhouette of a Lynx crossing on a narrow ledge. Life is abundant and evident in this majestic canyon around the clock.

Day two

Finally a good night of sleep. In spite of the constant roar of the river rushing by, the lack of sleep for the past few nights finally caught up with me. Up and bathed, I feel ready to meet another day. We have an interesting mix of folks on the trip this year. Half of the group came from Indiana with me (along with my son who is working as a gofer for the boat company) and the other half are from Colorado. We are working to try and mix up the group but there are some natural resistances to those efforts.

Today the hike to Saddle Canyon was long, hot and difficult. It was a good thing Ryan went on the walk with us because with his long legs, he was able to make it to the top of the huge bolder we need to climb to get to our goal. With him on top helping to pull everyone up, we all made it. We played in the little pools and then headed back to the boats.

We always try to make it to Nankoweap for our second night on the river. Nankoweap is probably the most magical place on the river from my perspective. High above the river, in the canyon wall are the Anasazi granaries. There are five little rooms that were constructed under and overhang with small stones. The hike up to the granaries is tough as it is probably 300-400 feet above the canyon floor. There is no technical climbing, just lots of sun and hundreds of switch-backs, thus you hike more than a mile uphill.

At river level there are hundreds of black collared lizards as well as their favorite food, black sand flies. The lizards will feed in the shady areas where the flies are and then run to a patch of sunlight to warm their bodies so they have enough energy to feed some more. Talk about nature's solar cells. Because this area gets a fair amount of moisture, there is considerable vegetation and plenty of lovely private spaces to set up one's campsite. I have one favorite spot that I discovered on my first trip and I always try to get it. Being the instructor in the course, however I do let others seek their spots first, but they usually do not find my little getaways and so I am usually able to get my favorite spots.

Nankoweap is one of the best places to fish for rainbow trout. The National Parks system does stock the river from time-to-time, but the trout are able to breed in the river as well. Even so, over the ten trips, I did see a decline in the population of fish. I also saw some trout that seemed to be a cross between the rainbow and the brown trout. Even so, they were delicious when stuffed with green peppers, onions and mushrooms and grilled on our cooking grill.

Day three

I like to get up early when I am at Nankoweap because the view of the sun descending the canyon wall is breathtaking. Camera set, I get several good shots before everyone is up and about. Day three is always a very busy day for us. This day, however was to have a less than pleasant start. We had all had breakfast and were loading the boats. I was on one boat and needed to get to the other. Since they were side-by-side, I planned to jump from the baloney tube of one to the baloney tube of the other. That was fine, but there was a lot of sand on the second tube which caused my feet to slide out from under me. I slid to the floor of the decking and my toe slammed under the flex joint but there was no room for the toenail. There was not much we could do except stop the bleeding and wrap the toe, knowing full well that with the first rapid the wrapping would be wet and fall off.

Mid-morning we made it to the junction with the Little Colorado River. The Little Colorado River is a beautiful aqua blue river that has extremely high levels of calcium sulfate that has leeched out of the rocks along the way. Because of the high salt content, it is like floating in salt water. The temperature is just right for a relaxing float, but it is important to wash off in the Colorado River to remove the calcium sulfate from your skin. With an open wound, it is not a good time for me to play in the river. Several presentations are made here because the rock shelves make a perfect classroom. Once we had taken our time here, we got back on the river.

Just downstream there is a sacred spot where the Anasazi and even some of the modern tribes come to to gather salt for the tribe. The long trek is a right of passage for warriors. In order to verify that they made the trip, they leave a petroglyph in the salt deposits on the cliff wall. Because this is sacred ground, we are not allowed to make contact with the shore. We can pull close, but no contact. The stories say that if you do violate the sacred space, something bad will happen to you. We had just finished telling the stories and our boat was just about to pull away from the area where we stopped, when an unexpected eddy caught our boat and swung us against a shore outcrop. We quickly backed away, but we had made contact with the shore.

Moving on downstream, we made our usual stop at Phantom Ranch. This is the place in the canyon where the mule trains come down. Visitors to the canyon can spend the night at the lodge. We always have folks have their postcards ready and we take them back to be stamped with the Phantom Ranch mark and the stamp stating it was carried out by mule. There are some beautiful streams that gently flow into the Colorado River here and they are warm and clean. Just lying in their current is relaxing.

Postcards delivered and stamped, we get back into the boats. Terry Johnson and Ryan were in the lead boat and they took off. Tom was making his final trip before being certified as a boatman and he seemed to be doing fairly well. That was until he bumped us into the sacred ground. The stories were about to be proven true. Just as we were pulling away from the shore at Phantom, the boatmen decided to switch fuel tanks. There are several images I want to create for you. First, there are two bridges over the river at this point, both were built for the mules, but the new bridge was made of an open grate. Clearly the engineer designing the new bridge did not know about hoofed animals and open grates. They can see through them and thus will not walk on them. As a result, the mules still use the old bridge and the park rangers walk across the new bridge. Secondly, just after you leave Phantom Ranch, the river takes a left bend and there is a major rapid right down stream. After the rapid there is another big bend in the river. We were just free floating around the first bend, waiting for the boatmen to restart the motor. They pulled and pulled and pulled on the cord, but the motor would not start. The rapid is sucking us downstream faster and faster. In a panic, they tried to reconnect the initial fuel tank (it was later discovered that we had been given a tank that had some water in it along with the gasoline.) As frantically as the men worked, the motor would not start and we were sucked into the rapid. Because we could not steer the boat we crashed into a large boulder sticking up in the river. Being resourceful, we felt we could bounce the boat off the rock if we all jumped in synchrony. I was out on the nose tube with nothing to hold onto and others were positioned forward to try and appropriately distribute the weight. We were successful in freeing ourselves from one rock, but another grabbed us as soon as we were free from the first.

By this time the other boat realized that we were not behind them so the came back upstream, not all that easy to do with only 25 horsepower. They stopped the boat in a small alcove downstream from the rapid while still beyond the bend. Everyone bailed out and climbed over a huge rock wall to see what was happening; everyone except Ryan, he was told to stay with the boat. Once Terry saw what was happening, he sent someone back to Ryan to tell him to watch for any bodies that might come floating downstream. If he saw anyone, he was to start up his boat and go after them. Keep in mind, Ryan had never piloted the boat through a rapid, and yes, there was another one just downstream. He had visions of having to try and rescue his own mother and that had this 18-year-old more than a little anxious.

There were factors working against us, we were too far away from shore to throw a line to shore and have everyone pull us off the rocks because there was too much weight in the boat. Secondly, the water level was going down at an alarming rate. This was Saturday afternoon and it takes 24 hours for the water to make it from Glenn Canyon Dam to Phantom Ranch, this means that we were getting Friday afternoon/evening's water outlet. The whole purpose of the Glenn Canyon Dam is to create hydroelectric power for the southwest. When businesses close down Friday afternoon, the need for electricity decreases, so the Dam lets less water out. Theoretically, we might have to wait two days for enough water to float the boat again.

About this time a park ranger walked across the new bridge and she saw what was happening. She came down to the beach where our folks from the other boat were standing and conferred with Terry. Since the rangers had just had an emergency evacuation training the previous week, she was eager to put things in motion. She radioed for a helicopter to see if we could rig a way to get the boat off the rocks. The helicopter came in and flew around us several times. He was so close you could almost see the pilot's whiskers. It is amazing that this should have happened where it did. To my knowledge, there are only two other locations in the entire 185 miles that we travel where a helicopter might be able to land, one is at Cardinas Gardens and the other is where we end our trip. Having scoped out the situation, the chopper landed on the sandy beach. By now, Ryan was told to anchor the boat and join the rest of the crew. He was relieved to see that I was still on the boat and not in the water. After consultation on shore, it was decided that everyone would be taken off the boat and we would spend the night there on the beach and determine what we would do the next day.

We were at a wide point in the canyon and the boat was perhaps 300 feet from the beach. There is only one way to get people off a boat, in the middle of a rapid. A park ranger went up with the chopper and was then lowered onto the boat wearing a screamer suit. The screamer suit is hooked by a carabineer hook to a long rope and then one is either lowered or raised by a pulley. The ranger was lowered onto the boat, took off the screamer suit and asked who wanted to be first. Remember I said we had an interesting mix on this trip and by day three we were finally getting some mixing of Midwesterners and westerners. Our oldest traveler was a mountain climbing 73 year old who jumped up and joyfully said he wanted to be first!! That set the tone for a few of the flat-landers who had a bit of acrophobia. Once he was safely on shore there was an eager lineup of rafters waiting their turn. Within 45 minutes I was being lifted off the boat. The only remaining person on the boat after the ranger left was Tom the boatman. He was to spend the night on the boat in case something should break free. As soon as I was out of my screamer suit Ryan was there pulling me into a big bear hug. He had been more affected by the 'what-ifs' than I have ever seen him.

Everyone on the beach was hugging and talking and more importantly sharing what they had with others. Half of us had our gear still on the boat and all of us had most of the food and cooking supplies on the boat in the river. The National Parks provided sleeping bags and "C-rations" for us. Everyone had all their needs met that night because of the generosity of their fellow travelers. The rangers left a deflated canoe and said good night. Theoretically they did not want us using their canoe, but we did nonetheless. With Ryan and TJ's good work, we were able to bring over the griddle and some food for breakfast. It was the best part of the trip to have everyone pulling together and all having a good night's sleep.

Day four

Early in the morning, before daylight, we began the process of taking off the boat bags from the stranded boat. By lessening the weight we were hopeful that the boat might float free, even if the water level was not supposed to come up. Ivo, TJ, Ryan and I had met the night before and decided that if the boat was not free by 9:00 a.m., we would have to take half of the folks out of the canyon by hiking the mule trail up to the top. Ryan and I would lead the folks out and we had selected the strongest campers to be the ones to hike out. It would not be an easy hike since we might be carrying our boat bags and it is a nine-mile hike up.

Everyone had had a good breakfast and all but one boat bag had made it off the boat. There was one bag that fell off the canoe and was somewhere down-stream. It was an orange bag and there were only two orange bags, a doctor's bag and mine. As it turned out, it was the doctor's bag that was free floating.

I was getting anxious about the conditions as it was almost 8:30 and I did not want to tell 15 people that their trip was over. I kept looking at the river and I could swear that the water level was coming up, but that was impossible since I had the 24-hour water outlet data. Even so, it sure looked like it was coming up. I got up with my list of those who were going to have to walk out of the canyon and as I did, I heard a wild and jubilant shout coming from the beach. The boat was free!!! Sunday morning, and the boat was free. We had fixed the motor the night before and soon the engine roared to life. Tom took the boat through the rapid and pulled up to the downstream end of the beach. Within minutes we were organized and began loading the boats. All in all we were only an hour and a half late getting on the river and a few miles upstream from where we should have been. Miracles happen even in the canyon. We made our peace with the Anasazi spirits and thanked them for not punishing us too much.

We had to shorten some of our visits on day four, but folks were working together and enjoying the camaraderie. We still had an orange boat bag to try and find, but there seemed to be no luck until we had gone about 19 miles downstream. All of a sudden I heard Ryan yell and point to an area of a rapid we were just about to go through. There on the edge of the rapid was one orange boat bag. As soon as we made it through the rapid, Ryan was able to hang over the end of the boat and lug the bag into the boat. What a roar of celebration went up from everyone. We had been challenged and we had survived. There were a few damp items in the bag, but basically the bag did exactly what it was supposed to do, it floated and kept things pretty safe. Tonight our campsite was near Deer Creek and everyone slept soundly.

Day five

We spent some time in the morning playing at Deer Creek and the pools that are tucked in the canyon walls. Our major goal for the day, however was Havasu. A few years ago a major late summer storm came through the area and devastated the reservation above and ravaged the riparian region below. This year there were signs that the vegetation was coming back and we were able to find the grottos that were nested under rock outcrops in the stream. Havasu is a wonderful place to play and this group was ready to play together today.

Back on the river we were able to make camp at Fern Glen which, as the name implies, is a fairyland of ferns.

Day six

Our last day leaves us with only fifteen miles of river to travel. Within those 15 miles, however we will encounter the fastest navigable white water in the Northern Hemisphere. Lava Falls Rapid drops 37' vertically over a distance of just a few hundred feet. It is ranked as a 10+ rapid. Before we get to Lava Falls we pass the Vulcan's Anvil, which is a lava plug in the middle of the Colorado River. Rafters toss coins at the Anvil for good luck in successfully navigating Lava Falls.

When we get to Lava Falls, we pull over to the shore and the boatmen walk along the boulders beside the river to survey the current condition of Lava Falls. The Grand Canyon is in a constant state of evolution and even between successive runs of the river significant changes can take place in how the major rapids flow. Once the survey is complete the first boat heads into the rapid. Those in the second boat can stay along the side and catch some photos of the first group. Now it is time for us to make the final run. We look for the V shaped tongue of the rapid that indicates the direction we should take. Tom hits the V head on and we hunker down for a wild ride. One miscue and we could crash into a huge boulder near the end of the rapid, but Tom does it right and we cheer the end of a successful run.

Just a few miles downstream we pull over to a wide beach area and remove all personal belongings from the boats. A quick lunch is prepared and soon the unmistakable whap, whap, whap of the chopper blades can be heard over the roar of the river. The helicopter that will take us out will carry 5-6 people per run. Over the next hour we all have the opportunity to see the canyon unfold beneath us as to head to Whitmore International Airport. The name implies far more than what is. It is a deserted dirt strip on top of a plateau with a 6x10' sun shade with one picnic table under the covering. We will board small prop planes to take us either back to Marble Canyon Lodge or to Las Vegas, depending upon the initial arrangements made. As we fly back to Marble Canyon Lodge, we can see all of the places we have been in the past six days. We may be going back to our old lives, but we will go back, changed individuals–renewed, refreshed, restored, and recreated.

15

Gaining Legitimacy

The evaluation from my boss at Anderson University that suggested I might not be a true scientist rankled me for quite a long time. My students all scored very well on graduate entrance exams in the subjects that I taught. I knew I was offering "good science." Still I knew the fact that I held an EdD rather than a PhD was holding me back. I had made the decision that it was time to look for opportunities to advance. I suspected that other institutions that did not know my ability in the laboratory/classroom would have some similar prejudices against me as a scientist. I began considering the advisability of going back to school to earn a PhD. After speaking with several colleagues at research I institutions, I received a common recommendation–that was, to not get a PhD on top of the EdD, but to do a post-doctoral research experience. The National Science Foundation (NSF) has a wonderful program whereby persons who have research grants can bring on inexperienced researchers, either from high schools or non-research colleges with the idea of giving them post-doctoral research experiences. The philosophy is that the research skills can then be taken back to the new researcher's home institution.

Dr. Steven Reynolds at Indiana University/Purdue University of Indianapolis (IUPUI) had one such NSF grant and he was graciously willing to go after the extra money to bring me into his research lab. It was somewhat of a comical situation because I was old enough to be the mother of most of his students and almost old enough to be Dr. Reynolds' mother. Even so, there was much I could learn from his research protocols and much I could teach his students about being productive and keeping good records. Steve was not sure how to interact with his students; supervision was new to him, so he turned them over to me. In turn, he taught me the techniques to proceed with his research project.

The post-doctoral tenure took place during the summer of 1993. That summer my son was working for ATA (American Trans-Air) in Indianapolis and I was driving to Indianapolis to do my post-doc. We were both out of the house by 6:00 a.m. It would have been nice if we had been able to car-pool, but Ryan spent his days at the Indianapolis airport and I began at IUPUI, ran the labs and conducted my experiments until about 3:30 p.m. and then drove to Anderson University to spend a few hours taking care of department head activities and to oversee the major renovation/construction project that was taking place in our building. We were adding an addition to the building and significantly gutting the inside of the older portion, creating refurbished labs and new offices. My responsibility was to oversee the entire construction process. Keep in mind, department heads at Anderson University were only on 10 month contracts but were expected to work in the summer to do any planning that would be necessary for the coming school year–this without compensation.

That summer Nicole was also working at a local restaurant, so we were all away from home during the daytime. I would get home around 6:30 p.m., fix dinner and interact with the kids for a short while and then crash. Ryan was much the same. The 90-minute drives into Indianapolis might be for some folks, but neither Ryan nor I relished them.

By the end of the summer I had gained significant laboratory research experience that would allow me to bring back the experiences and techniques to my students at Anderson University. The problem, however was that Anderson did not have the equipment necessary for me to continue with the research I had been doing at IUPUI. I did a bit of investigating and discovered that Ely Lilly had a warehouse filled with cast-off scientific equipment. They allowed schools to propose what they needed and how it would be used. It did not take long for me to have a proposal in their hands and all I needed to do was rent a very large moving truck to pick up the items in Indianapolis. With a few student helpers in tow, I drove the large moving truck to Lilly's to pick up the equipment that would further our opportunities to do research. With everything loaded onto the truck we were on our way back to Anderson. One piece of equipment, a super cooled freezer, could not be brought up to the second floor until we had the new elevator installed and operational, but the remainder of the equipment was put into place in my new research lab. Over the next year and a half, I was able to engage many students in the process of conducting true research and it was exciting for all of us. There was considerable skepticism on the part of my colleagues, I suspect in part because they were not doing research, but I knew the experiences would be invaluable for the students.

Many of my professional colleagues knew that I had gone back to do a post-doc and as a result, I was asked to represent the National Association of Biology Teachers (NABT) on the National Research Council's Chair's Advisory Council. The NRC council was responsible for the development of the *National Science Education Standards*. The council consisted of the executive directors of eight other national societies and myself. The fact that the executive director of another organization asked for me to represent NABT, spoke volumes about his appreciation of my scientific knowledge. I would serve on the NRC Chair's Advisory Council from 1993-1999. Every six weeks I would fly to Washington DC for a daylong meeting. When I moved to California, of course it took more than a day out of my schedule, but it was worth the involvement. It was heady business to know that you and seven or eight other people were leading the larger team that would impact all of science education in this nation for decades to come. The NRC's *National Science Education Standards* has become the model for the national standards in many other disciplines in the country. On more than one occasion I would be sitting in a Washington DC conference room waiting for things to get started and thinking, Wow! Who would have thought that little girl exploring the Wisconsin woods would be in the Nation's capital setting standards for generations of children to come.

Without a doubt, my involvement with the NRC Standards played a major role in my being selected to become the Dean of Mathematics, Science & Engineering at Fresno City College in 1995. It was also a factor; I am sure, to my being named a Fellow of the American Association for the Advancement of Science in 2001.

I was taking a risk to jump into the post-doctoral adventure, but it was a risk that has paid off time after time. I was not afraid to look like a fool when I first went into Steve's lab and I was not afraid to let the other students teach me how to do some of the procedures. There was a rich give and take in the lab and I would like to think that I left the lab in better shape when I left, than it was when I arrived. I do know that through my experiments, I was able to identify one protein that had not previously been identified and that felt good for this old dog.

16

California Dreaming–the Nightmare

Ryan had graduated from Purdue University, Nicole was successfully moving through her courses at Purdue. I had progressed as far as I could at Anderson University and it was time for me to look for an opportunity to advance. I had my post-doctoral experience behind me, had taken my sabbatical and now I needed a new challenge.

One day I was on the phone with a friend in California talking about an organization to which we both belonged. At the end of the conversation he said, "We really need your expertise here in California." I indicated that I had not lost anything in CA; besides, I could not afford to live in CA. He was quick to note that if you lived interior to the coasts, housing was very affordable. I countered that there has to be a job and he reminded me if I checked the *Chronicle of Higher Education* I would likely find several jobs. Because I was eager for a change, I checked the *Chronicle* that afternoon. To my amazement, there was a Dean position at Fresno City College. Specifically, it was the Associate Dean of Instruction/Dean of the Division of Mathematics, Science & Engineering. This was early March and I thought why not. I submitted my application and basically forgot it.

When I did not hear from FCC I assumed that I would spend my 19th year at Anderson University. There was a group of faculty and staff was going to Tahiti the summer of 1995 and I decided to give myself a 50th birthday present and go on the trip. A few weeks before the trip, I received a call from Fresno City College inviting me to come for an interview. The kicker was that it had to be on a certain date and I was slated to arrive in Tahiti on that day. I asked if there could be any leniency on the date and was told no, but they would do a phone interview–while I was in Tahiti. Anderson University was a wonderful school, but at that point in time it was rather paternalistic and they did not like people to leave them. Since I had no idea what the outcome would be of the interview, I did not want to jeopardize my job by telling anyone. As a result, I was forced to stretch the truth a little. When everyone was going on the "around the island" tour, I said that I had to take care of a business call, but would join everyone after their tour.

The first hour of the interview was with the search committee. I was in a beautiful paradise and the breezes were floating in through the window and I was in shorts and very comfortable. I was actually enjoying the process. The second hour of interviewing was with the President of the College. When he got on the phone he was being kind and said that I must feel like I was being raked over the coals. My response was that I was looking across the lanai to the tide-pools where they were seining for fish–it was very relaxing. With a laugh he said, "Be quiet, one of us is in the wrong place." Needless to say, the remainder of the interview went very well.

Again I pretty well dismissed the event and continued with my vacation. Because it was so expensive to call back and forth from the islands, Nicole and I had agreed that we would not call each other unless there was an emergency. About six or seven days into our trip, we were all on the island of Moorea at the Bali Hai resort. It was a charming place and the SCUBA diving had been good. One afternoon, as I was about to head out to the beach, there was a knock on the door. The young man handed me a note saying to call home. This mother's heart began to pound and I was extremely anxious. The only place to find a phone was in the lobby of the resort. I headed to the phone and found about a dozen of my fellow travelers waiting for me. They had heard the call come in and were concerned for me and were waiting to support me if something bad had happened. I was able to reach Nicole and she immediately said, "Mom, don't worry. Fresno City College just wants you to stop there on your way back from Tahiti." Okay, here are all of these concerned folks who don't know I am looking for a job, waiting to console me. I had to be very non-descript in my half of the conversation, yet I needed to know what kind of schedule there would be and there needed to be hotel, car and flight adjustments. My wonderful daughter had taken care of everything already. When I got off the phone I simply told the folks that the call I had taken days before was leading to some additional consultation.

After the vacation we landed in LA and I headed up to Fresno. Since I was definitely not planning on a job interview, I was not prepared with an appropriate wardrobe. There was a small mall near the hotel and I put a dent in my credit card getting ready for the interviews. The first day I met with the committee, the Chancellor, and a host of other individuals. The next morning I met with the Vice President and the President and then back to the Vice President. Before I left, I had been offered the job. I asked for 24 hours to make my decision.

I drove back to LA and caught the red-eye back to Indiana. On my drive back to Muncie, I got on my cell phone and told my Dean that I needed to talk with him. There was still a chance to stay at Anderson, but there had to be some movement on their part to keep me. When I told my Dean of the offer to become the Dean of Mathematics, Science & Engineering his only response was "You gotta do what you gotta do." My response back to him was, "Then I guess you have made my decision for me." When I got to my home I call Fresno and told them I was coming–in three weeks!!!

Shortly after taking the position, I attended the annual meeting of the National Association of Biology Teachers (NABT). One of my friends congratulated me on my new job and said, "Do you know how few of you there are?" I did not know what she was referring to so I said, "How few of me what?" Her response was, "Women Deans of Mathematics, Science and Engineering." That got me very curious and I began to dig to find the answer. As best I could tell, there were only about 12 of us women deans of mathematics, science and engineering. I suppose when you throw in the engineering, it eliminates a significant number of women. I suspect if you talk with any of the engineering faculty at FCC, they would have no complaints about my ability to deal with the discipline of engineering. I proudly wear a shattered glass pin from the National Women's Political Caucus that represents having broken through the glass ceiling. It is a special remembrance of what possibility thinking and dogged determination can do. Often I am complemented on the pin, when I wear it–it is rather stunning. When asked, I will share what its meaning is and the fact that anyone can succeed with some skill and determination.

While in California I was invited to be a featured speaker at a conference. They wanted me to speak about being a woman in a non-traditional role. I offered them something even better–a mother-daughter team. Both of us have chosen the path less traveled. Nicole is brighter than I could ever hope to be. She graduated from Purdue University in Civil Engineering with a perfect 4.0 grade point average and is now a successful structural engineer with her PE license in Denver, Colorado. Not surprisingly, the presentation was very well received.

The faculty and staff of the Division of Mathematics, Science and Engineering were so welcoming and so eager to have someone on board. For the first time, I would be working with a group of folks who never doubted my credibility as a scientist. Even before moving to CA, my secretary Carmen and her husband offered me the use of a home they owned until I could get into the home I purchased. Carmen and Klaus Caldwell were the most wonderful friends one could have; they showed me so many sides of Fresno and introduced me to many of their friends as well as their own family. Being so far away was made easier because of these two loving folks.

There were many outstanding folks at Fresno City College. From my dear friend Adrian I learned all about the cultivation of almonds, from Dona I learned about deep friendships that lift up people, from Julie I learned the unconditional joy of life. While I do not see myself as a feminist, I think I was able to encourage some of the women in the Division to believe in themselves and to reach for better things. I am pleased to say that my replacement is a woman I handpicked and she is doing great things in the Division.

This was my only foray into community colleges and it was an adventure and important to my future career. Because my background was at the college/university levels, I found I missed the intellectual stimulation that comes from folks doing research. I do know that commitment on the part of the community college faculty I had the pleasure of working with, could not be matched. They taught me much about giving of time and I believe I was able to teach them how to dream dreams. I was in California at the right time–there was money!! This meant that we were able to do things that they had not been able to do previously. I think we strengthened the programs and provided students and faculty with new equipment that allowed them to compete with the four-year programs.

More than helping them to rediscover the ability to dream dreams, I think I created a sense of community where there had been none. One of the first faculty members I had the opportunity to meet was James Ross. James is a gorgeous southern gentleman and mathematician who, at one point had been an excellent tennis player. There was a young woman who had been his student about 11 years before I met James. She was emotionally unbalanced and when James suggested that she seek counseling, she became upset. They left his office and got into the elevator with another student. The distraught student pulled a gun from her backpack and fired at James, severing his lower spine. She also shot at the other student who held up her microbiology text which stopped the bullet, and then she turned the gun on herself, killing herself all in the time it took to go from the third floor of the building to the first. When I met James he was confined to a wheelchair. He was going to be taking a medical leave my first semester as Dean because the use of his slide board to get into and out of his car was causing pressure sores. My question to the folks in the Division was why had no one campaigned to get James a handicap van so he could drive himself and not have to have an attendant or the slide board. They just had never thought of doing something like that. I asked James for his permission, and after considering it, finally said yes. A month later we had raised enough money to convert a van for his use. From that point on, I think the members of our division had a better understanding of community. Not that they were perfect, but better.

Not everything was sunshine in Fresno. On May 27, 1997, I was getting ready to go with a group from the Fresno Community Chorus on a tour of France and Israel. We would be leaving in a day or so, but on that day something happened that would affect me for the next several years. While at my office, I received a phone call from one of the homicide detectives from the Fresno Police. He wanted to ask me some questions about one of my adjunct faculty members. A few days earlier a woman who owned a used bookstore near the campus had been murdered and my adjunct faculty member was the prime suspect. He had claimed to be in our office area making copies at the time of the murder. Since I had been in my office all that day and had even worked late, I knew that he had not been in the area making copies as he claimed. The detective asked some more questions and I gave him some information that he did not know. At the end of the conversation he asked if I owned a gun. I was stunned by the question and told him that I did not have one. He then asked if I would consider getting a gun, and again I said no, but this time I asked why. He said "If.... did commit this murder, you are the next one on his list." I did not know what to say. The detective would, in subsequent conversations tell me that this individual hated his mother and blamed everything wrong in his life on her. He transferred that hate to any woman who might be in a position to make decisions about his life, like his boss. Truly, I believe that I was in a bit of shock with the news.

I went home that afternoon to welcome a longtime friend from Muncie who was in California on business and was going to stay at my home while he conducted his business. How do you deal with being a gracious hostess while you are trying to process the fact that someone may be out to kill you? It was probably the best and the worst time that he could have been in my home. Because we were friends and able to talk about anything, his strength calmed me for the time being, it was what I needed.

Thankfully the adjunct faculty member self selected to not teach while the investigation was ongoing, but he was in my office many times trying to tell me what to say to the police. For three and a half of the five and a half years I was in California he stalked me. It started with the visits to the office and then there were the twin drawings of male genitalia that showed up on my garage door one Saturday morning. I later learned that they were the same drawings left at the scene of the murder. This individual also followed me down the street at night as I walked my dogs. He was in his car with the lights off. There were also numerous break-in attempts at my home. Each event would happen at 3-6 month intervals. As a result I never slept through the night; I would hear every noise in the house, in my yard, everywhere.

For the first year I just did not know how to cope with the tensions and the fear. During the day I had to function effectively in my job. I was reasonably safe at work since our police force knew about the situation and watched for this person to come on campus. On those occasions when we knew he would be coming to see me, there was always a police officer waiting out of sight. It was a horrible way to live! Finally I had a conversation with the school psychologist. I needed to know if my fear and the tendency to spend my nights crying was a normal reaction to this kind of tension. He assured me that it was, but said if I wanted some drugs to help me sleep, they could be prescribed. Sleeping too soundly was the last thing I wanted, so no drugs.

After the incident of being followed, I finally agreed to get a gun. I have never liked guns and never wanted one around where a child might be able to get to it and get hurt. Since I was alone for the most part, I decided to get the gun. I was not about to have a gun, however if I did not know how to properly use it. I signed up for a class and showed up on the assigned Saturday morning. There were five or six men in the class and myself. One of the men was a member of the College's Student Disabilities Advisory Council; the others were all police officers being recertified. The instructor asked what kind of gun I had and I told him a Taurus. He wanted to see it and commented that it looked like it had never been fired. I confirmed that it had not, nor had I ever shot any gun. You could hear a collective groan coming from the men in the class. You could almost hear them thinking "dumb blond—we are going to have to wait for her." The classroom portion of the class completed, we headed out to the firing range. The targets were in place and I was invited to join one of the men to shoot first. Our targets were male silhouettes and in the first round of shots I did not miss my target or the region were told to shoot for. There were more than a few surprised grunts coming from the men. On our second round we were a little further away and again I never missed. At each distance I hit my mark. Finally one of the men wanted to know if I was working under cover for the police department to be sure they were doing their jobs. I laughed and assured them that I was who I claimed to be. Thankfully the one man I knew vouched for me. One of them finally recognized my name and said, "Oh yea, you are the one with the stalker." Word was clearly around in the department. When we were about finished, I asked if I could try a rapid fire round. I figured that under pressure that might be a more likely scenario. Once again, I could say that I just did not miss. Actually, I need to qualify that statement. There were two holes in my target that were not totally within the silhouette, but had the silhouettes been anatomically correct, the man would have been missing an ear and part of his family jewels. What can I say, my eye-hand coordination is good!

When I finally moved to Pennsylvania, I sold my gun and I have slept through the night without fear. Rarely do noises alarm me, every once in a while a noise will take me back to California and for a few brief moments my heart will race, then I remember where I am and smile.

17

Out of California

While in California I had the privilege of meeting many wonderful people. My secretary Carmen Caldwell and her husband Klaus were my salvation in Fresno. Even before I moved to California they were offering their friendship and their help. While I had found a home fairly quickly, I could not get into it for several months, so Carmen and Klaus rented a home to me. They included me in family Thanksgiving dinners and more. One could not have truer friends then Carmen and Klaus. There were others as well.

California is a beautiful state and I had an opportunity to hone my photography skills. I know that when I do finally retire, I will likely spend even more time with that art medium. Beautiful vistas, stunning swimming pool and the agreeable weather to go with it, good friends all were not enough to make up for the stalker. I began my search for a new position. Much like what happened with my finding the Fresno job, I had been corresponding with a friend from Pittsburgh and they encouraged me to consider Pennsylvania. I had never considered Pennsylvania, but I knew that it was a gorgeous state that I had driven through on many occasions. On Friday July 13, 2000 I checked the electronic version of the Chronicle of Higher Education. Amazingly there was a posting that would appear in the July 20th print edition for the CEO and Dean of Penn State Berks-Lehigh Valley College. The only problem was that it said the closing date was July 5, 2000. I called to see what was happening and was told that they had had some significant delays and that was the cause of the mix-up. They were interested and asked that I send my information as soon as possible. I sent an electronic application that day and by Tuesday they were calling back asking if they could check my references.

The next week I was back in the Midwest for a family reunion. Nicole and I had flown into Indiana, she to visit her grandparents and dad and I to visit some friends. From there we drove up to Michigan. On the way, I checked my phone messages at home. There was a call from Penn State and I tried to call them back. We were driving through some of the farmland of Michigan and I kept loosing the cellular signal. I finally had Nicole pull over when I got a strong signal and leaned that they wanted me to fly out to Philadelphia for an airport interview. Since I was coming all the way from California they flew me in the day before the interview and flew me back the day after the interview. I did take a quick drive up to Reading to see what housing might look like. I did not see anything initially promising, but that would later change.

The interview was held in one of the meeting rooms of the USAirways Club. The committee conducted 14 interviews over two days, which had to be grueling to say the least. I had the distinction of being last—always the best place in higher education interviews. Several weeks passed and school was underway at FCC. Finally in September I received the call inviting me to come for a two and a half day interview in October. I had my choice of going first, middle or last. Knowing that I had the choice meant that I was pretty high on their list and of course I chose last. I was slated to give a presentation at NABT in Orlando, FL in October, so I arranged to fly from Orlando to Pennsylvania for the interviews. This was really to my advantage as I had had a few days to adjust to the Eastern time zone.

I flew to Allentown, Pennsylvania on a Sunday. I was scheduled to start early on Monday morning, but the person picking me up thought we might want to have our initial interview that evening, thus giving me a little more of a chance to be ready for her campus. Dr. Ann Williams was, and still is, the CEO of the Penn State Lehigh Valley campus and we seemed to hit it off immediately. She also learned rather quickly that I am flexible. We went to a restaurant for dinner. We both ordered a glass of Merlot and just jumped into a lively conversation. I knew that there were some difficulties resulting from the merger of the Berks (Reading) campus and the Lehigh Valley campus. Soon the waitress came to put something on the table and in the process, knocked my glass of Merlot into my lap. I had planned to wear the jacket the next day, but that was out of the question. Lots of towels, soda water and laughter later, we did all we could for the jacket and went on with our conversation. Bless her heart, she took the jacket to a cleaner the next morning and had it back to me by the afternoon.

All that Monday I had interesting conversations with the faculty and staff of the Lehigh Valley. Late that afternoon I was driven to Reading. The next day was to be a true test of my endurance. Beginning with a 7:30 a.m. breakfast meeting and not ending until late that night, I had more than enough opportunities to demonstrate grace under fire. At mid afternoon, I was scheduled to give a general presentation about my vision for the college. The presentation was scheduled in a large theater style classroom. I had been introduced and was just getting started when this lost looking, short, older man shuffled into the front of the room. Clearly he looked confused, so I introduced myself to him and asked if I could help him. He said he had come to hear the possible new Dean. I told him he was in exactly the right place and invited him to have a seat in the front. In this room were more than just the faculty and staff of the college, but also the Vice Provost and his assistant who had flown down in the University plane to hear me and to take me back to University Park. The Vice Provost was about to get up and get rid of this intruder, but watching me interact with this sweet man had him sitting down again. Once the older gentleman was settled I went right back to what I had been sharing with the assembled group.

I have heard people say that you can measure the true character of a person by the way they treat people who cannot help them. I had no idea who this man was, nor did 99% of the people in the room. They liked the way I gently guided this confused man. The one percent who knew who the man was, knew I had just made a significant friend. As it turns out, this wonderful man was one of the college's more significant donors. My interaction with him that day was to be one of the last interactions where he was aware of what was going on around him. While Alzheimer's disease took away his memory and balance, he always retained his sense of humor and gentle spirit. Joe Boscov was laid to rest in July of 2004 and the memorial service was a true celebration of the gentle spirit and sharp intellect that all had known. The family will always be good friends to the college and to me.

There was stimulating give and take with the assembled group that afternoon and I felt alive and delighted to be a part of the process. From that event I was whisked off to the airport where we boarded the University plane. The Vice Provost's Administrative Assistant had been so incredibly helpful in making all of the arrangements for my trip and it was wonderful to have an opportunity to chat with her and to get her perspective of working for Penn State.

Once at University Park, we headed to a beautiful English inn where we met with the Provost and his wife, the Vice Provost and his wife, and another campus college Dean and his wife. Hors d'oeuvres and wine were served by the fireplace in the library—along with wonderful conversation. We were then lead to our private dining room where a sumptuous dinner was served. As anyone who has gone through interviews knows, you never have much of a chance to eat. I knew I had to eat something or I would not make it through the night. Somehow I made it through the evening without sounding too much like an idiot. The next morning I was not at all sure what I had said—not because of the alcohol consumed (I know how to sip) but because of the level of exhaustion. The next morning the Provost assured me that I was totally lucid the entire evening.

The third day was to be with many of the most senior personnel of the University. Each person was genuinely interested in me and what I saw for the future of the college, heady stuff. Finally I met with the president, Dr. Graham Spanier. Again, I had this wonderful sense of a real team and that the top level truly valued all who were a part of the team. Interviews completed, I was sent back to the airport to begin my trek back to Fresno.

It is extremely rare for me to sleep on an airplane, but I know I did sleep for part of the trip home. I was one exhausted pup!! Once home I got online and began looking at possible homes, I was that convinced that I had nailed the interviews. The week after my visit, there was a message from Dr. Erickson, the Provost, inviting me to call him the next day—the three-hour time difference wreaks havoc on coast-to-coast communications. I felt fairly sure of the nature of the conversation, but still, one never can tell. Sleep that night was impossible. By 5:00 a.m. the next morning I was on the phone, talking with the Provost. We were a few minutes into the call when he stopped and said, "What time is it there?" I just replied that it was early and there was no way I was going to wait any longer, we both laughed. The offer of employment was made and accepted in a matter of minutes. The difficult thing was they really wanted me as soon as possible. We agreed that I would arrive the end of January 2001.

This conversation took place the first week of November. I notified the folks at Fresno City College and then made plans to put my house on the market. The day before Thanksgiving the house was listed and 10 hours later sold for the full asking price. This was excellent news as that gave me a greater comfort level when I flew back to Pennsylvania the next weekend to look for a house.

I had spent considerable time online looking at what was for sale. There was one house in particular that I was convinced would be the one I would buy. The price was great and it looked good in the little photo that was posted. It was not exactly in the direction I wanted to be, but not too far off, either. I flew in on a Friday evening and the realtor had me slated to look at 14 houses Saturday, eight on Sunday and Monday was a carry over in case I did not find anything. We started out at 8:30 a.m. on Saturday with the house I was convinced I would buy. That was smart move on her part because once we walked into the home and were hit with a wall of cigarette smoke; I had to eliminate that home. I am allergic to cigarette smoke and yes, you can eventually get rid of the smell, but it would necessitate a lot of work before moving in. Since the floor plan would never work for entertaining, I was mentally able to let go of that house. By 10:30 a.m. I had gone through 10 of the 14 houses and the realtor was beginning to panic. I could walk into a home and know within a minute or two if it had any potential. She had two houses scheduled for the afternoon that were across from each other. One of the houses was vacant and the other she called to see if she could move the appointment up. Since the folks had just shown it, they were delighted to show it again and then have the rest of the day to themselves. The two homes were a bit above what I wanted to pay, but we walked into the vacant home first. I walked into the foyer with a harlequin tile floor, could see the two story glass wall ahead in the family room, turned left into the living room and asked the realtor "How low will they go?" I was done looking! She asked if I did not want to see the rest of the home and of course I did, but I knew this was the home I wanted. The home across the street was lovely, the same square footage and the same two acres of land, but it was $30,000 less than the one I wanted. It did not have the floor plan I needed, so it would not work, but it served as the perfect justification to offer a comparable price. Within two hours the offer was made and accepted. Not too bad for a house hunting expedition.

On January 25, 2001 I signed the papers for my new home and began work at Penn State Berks-Lehigh Valley College on January 29, 2001. From the beginning I have said that I cannot imagine a better job. There are challenges, of course, but the faculty, staff and administration is so competent, so interesting, and so committed to the students that I feel as though I have been completed professionally.

Before moving to Berks County, I was forewarned that Berks Countians tend to be very cold and unwelcoming. I am not sure if it is because of my position or my natural friendliness, but that warning has been anything but true. I have been welcomed into the community with open arms. A group of executive women have taken me into their fold and we have a grand time together. Additionally I was named by the Girl Scouts as one of three Women of Distinction for Berks County for 2003. The Chamber of Commerce has asked that I be one of the Women in Leadership speakers and the Governor has asked that I assist with the First Governor's Conference for Women. All in all, this is a wonderful place to be.

18

Hop Little Bunny

Maybe I should introduce Samantha. Samantha is my 5-year old Golden Retriever who thinks she is still 2. Actually, I have been told that Goldens tend to stay puppy like through much of their lives. She is a sweet tempered lover of a dog. Like a true Retriever, she will fetch a stick, ball, toy or snowball for hours on end if you have the endurance. Her all time favorite, however is the Frisbee. She knows no stranger and always is ready to play with anyone or anything. Her boyfriend Ryker lived across the street until recently and he would blow through their invisible fence and ours to come and play with Samantha. They would have a grand time, but I suspect he just loved coming over to take some of Samantha's toys from the yard. Every now and then we would receive a bag of replacement toys from Ryker as a peace offering for those that he had taken, and likely shredded. Though the neighbors have moved, Samantha still sits on the hip of our hill, by the road looking across the road for her pal.

The hour was late and I was exhausted. I had just had dinner with a special friend. While he has not yet discovered that I am the best thing that ever happened to him, we do still get together from time to time to have dinner or to go to a concert or football game. The conversation as always was delightful. We have an ease with each other that allows us to discuss politics, religion, serious matters and silly things. There is a rhythm to our time together, we laugh, we empathize, we encourage each other and we laugh some more. It always ends with some serious kissing, but nothing else except a deep desire for more. It will just have to wait. In any event, I made it home and then made my way up to bed, but I heard Samantha scratching at something and could not figure out what she was doing. I should say that usually Samantha is a quiet dog. Once the lights are out, she knows it is time to settle down and sleep so the noise coming from downstairs was unusual.

The next morning Samantha and I went out to get the paper. She usually walks me to the end of the driveway by having both of us hold onto a stick of her choice. Once back in the house, I sat on my loveseat in front of my fireplace. I had not been there long when Samantha began to scratch under the furniture. She has trained me to respond to certain stimuli. She takes a toy and shoves it under a couch or loveseat and then barks for me to come and get it out. I resist, but she is persistent and usually I come to retrieve the toy. The morning in question she did not so much bark, but growled a little. Her football was in front of the loveseat and I tossed it for her, but she stayed there on her belly looking under the loveseat. Finally I got down on my hands and knees to see what was under there. I did not see a toy, but still she whined and persisted. I knew there was no reading the paper until I got up and moved the loveseat, so I put the paper down and walked behind the loveseat. I slid the loveseat forward and was totally surprised to see a little baby bunny; perhaps 5 inches long huddled in the fringe of my oriental rug.

It looked as if the bunny was still alive, so I took Samantha with me to the kitchen to get a plastic container and lid. I did not want her frightening the bunny any more than it was, so I had to keep her with me. At this point I realized that she had probably brought the bunny in the night before and was hoping to play with it, but it scurried under the loveseat and stayed there all night. I took the plastic container and placed it over the bunny and it tried to jump a little. Ever so slightly I lifted one edge and slid the lid under the container and the bunny. I tried to take it to where I thought the parents might be. Unfortunately Samantha got to the site just when I did, so she knew where I was putting the bunny.

It is relevant to note that our neighborhood is overrun with rabbits. Every spring and early summer I have to take care as I crest the hill on the way to my home. There are usually a dozen or more rabbits of various ages hopping across the street.

After depositing the bunny in some ground cover, I took Samantha back in the house with me to give the bunny a chance to hide. Samantha was not to be deterred. Within minutes she was back out to the drop-off point and with her keen sense of smell, she was successful in finding her new best friend. Now if the bunny understood that all Samantha wanted to do was to play with it, it would not have been nearly as frightened, but if a predator that is perhaps 20 times your size takes you in their mouth, it is pretty difficult to focus on the gentleness with which they are holding you.

By the time Samantha found her new best friend, I was getting ready to mow. She brought her new buddy down to the lower garage to show me and she gently placed the bunny on the ground close to where I was. I knew the bunny was still alive, so I started throwing a stick for Samantha. To a Golden there is nothing better than chasing a good stick, so she went bounding after the stick. After throwing the stick about a dozen times, the bunny decided it was safe to make a get-away. It hopped over to a woodpile and hid there. Samantha sensed that her buddy was not where she had left it and began sniffing for the trail. I thought the bunny was safe and headed out on the mower. I had not made more than one round on my two acres when I saw Samantha with something in her mouth. She had dug the bunny out of the woodpile. At this point, the poor bunny did what all terrified bunnies do, its heart just stopped.

Samantha gently laid the bunny in the mulch and continued to softly bump it with her nose, as if to encourage it to awaken. It was, of course not going to move then or ever again. Ultimately Samantha realized that her new best buddy was no longer of this world and she carefully buried the bunny in the mulch. This was touching, but I have a feeling that I may some day see this bunny again. Samantha has a habit of burying those items she treasures the most and then digs them up at a later date when they have had time to decompose a bit. They make a lovely presentation on my white carpets. She is such a generous dog!

19

Never Too Old To Learn

My goal is to learn something new each day. There are times when I have to learn something a few days in a row, before I realize that I have already learned that, but learning is part of my life mission—my learning and the opportunity for others to learn. Not every lesson is a welcome one. Some lessons come from not doing one's homework and some from stupidity. Other learning experiences are sheer serendipity. What follows are a few selected learning experiences.

First Lesson: I know someone is watching over me.

In the early 1980's I was gaining in recognition for my work with science education and science education reform. I was quite surprised when I received an invitation to be a featured speaker at a conference to be held in India. The conference conveners were hopeful that they would be funded by the India government. They were offering to pay my airfare and provide a modest honorarium. Accepting the offer was a no-brainer. There was also a remote possibility that I would do some corporate scouting for a neighbor who owned all of Greeks Pizzerias in the country (or the franchises.) He had been thinking of opening a shop in New Delhi and was willing to pay to have me check things out there. I updated my passport, began working on my presentation, and made my airline reservation for a Pan Am flight. I began to get a bit concerned when I did not hear from the conference folks. Finally I did get a letter from them saying that they had not gotten the funding they had hoped for, but the conference would still go on—could I pay my own way? Two thousand dollars for a flight was just not in the budget nor did my neighbor want to foot that kind of bill, so I declined the invitation. This was in the day when you could make an airline reservation and actually cancel it without penalty. I did not think anything about the missed opportunity until the evening of the day I was supposed to be flying to India. That night on the news it was announced that the very flight that I had booked had exploded over the Atlantic. Had the money been there, I would not be here.

That was not the only time when I have felt that the hand of God has intervened, there have been many times when I have felt that there is a purpose for my life, sometimes I might not be totally aware of the purpose, but I sense that I am driven to do what I do. The most recent example of a "saving grace" will be seen in the last lesson mentioned in this chapter.

Second Lesson: Humor is regional.

I did not realize just how regional humor, or a sense of humor can be. I grew up in the Midwest and the humor there is rather earthy. Of course one needed to be situation specific. You would not choose a more ribald comment at a formal dinner, but just might be a little bolder when you were amongst good friends. Midwesterners are salt of the earth folks who will give you the shirt off their backs if it is needed. They also are very trusting. It takes a great deal to get a Midwesterner to distrust you and this fact will be used in another lesson later on.

Californians are more likely to be up on the latest online joke and they often will center their humor around the change of weather or the lack of earthquakes in their particular region.

Humor on the east coast is a bit more subtle, okay, make that a lot more subtle. I am still trying to learn when someone is kidding me or being serious. I really did not figure these differences out until I used my Midwest humor on the east coast. To set the stage, I really love what I am doing with Penn State. It is a great place to work and the opportunity to have a significant impact on the growth of a young college within the University is truly fulfilling. Shortly after I had gotten settled into the job, I was talking with a few friends, now these are folks whom I feel very comfortable around and so I allowed my Midwestern humor to slip out— bad idea. One person asked how things were going with the job and my response was, "if it was any better it would be orgasmic." I expected a chuckle. You know what happens when you drop a medicine ball on the floor? There is a loud thud and it just lays there, well that was the response I got from my midwestern humor. I certainly did not use that line again!!

Third Lesson: Trust is regional

As I mentioned previously, Midwesterners have a tendency to assume the best of folks and they will trust people until they prove themselves untrustworthy. This, I have learned is not a universal perspective on humanity.

I had been in California a few months and we were in the process of working with search committees to hire some new faculty members. I had done this before at Anderson University and it was familiar ground, or so I thought. During one meeting we were trying to push a timeline and I offered to make the background checks. Keep in mind, I was the Dean of this division and the other members of the search committee were faculty members. One of the faculty members had a knee jerk reaction to what I thought was an innocuous offer. She was adamant that the faculty members should make the calls and acted very upset that I would even consider saying what I had. Now this made absolutely no sense to me.

That evening I replayed the event over and over in my mind trying to understand why I had gotten such a strong reaction from this faculty member. The only explanation that I could come up with was that she did not trust me. I was already doing some good things for the Division and I thought folks were happy with my presence. I did not know what I could have done to lose her trust. When that thought formulated, I realized that I had likely just hit upon the answer. The next morning I sought her out and asked her to help me understand something that took place the previous day. I couched my comments in the fact that I was still learning not only the California culture, but the community college culture and I needed to understand as much as possible. I shared with her that when I was growing up, people trusted others until they proved themselves untrustworthy. If someone did not trust another initially, but waited until that person proved their trustworthiness, then they might have a reaction much like she had had the previous day. And so I asked her if that was what created her reaction. She was frank with me and said that was exactly where her reaction came from. She did not know me well enough to trust me yet and since no one was to be trusted until they proved themselves, she reacted as she had. I then asked if she thought her reaction was typical of her, Fresno, or perhaps all of California. I had been reading the papers and I had an idea of how she would respond. Her statement that that was pretty typical of all Californians confirmed what I suspected.

So where does that put easterners? I am not sure, but it appears that there is more of a mix in the east. There are those who hold back until they have measured your character, and there have been those who have embraced me without reservation. I do know that I have never lived in a more philanthropically minded community than Reading and Berks County.

Fourth Lesson: There is goodness everywhere you go.

As divorces go, ours was incredibly civil. Both Joe and I are decent people and I think that we truly wanted what was best for the other. There were many people who did not even know we had been divorced. One person however decided it was his mission to "punish" me for not staying married. This individual had been one of my physicians and we had become friends with he and his wife. We socialized together and they had been in our home as many times as we had been in their home. It was their habit to have a major summer party and we had always attended. When Joe and I were going through the divorce, he lived in our home until he could find another place to live. One afternoon this doctor called and asked for Joe. I told him that I did not expect him until that evening. The doctor proceeded to say, "Would you tell him that we want to invite HIM to our party in two weeks?" The message was clear, I was the outcast and Joe was in. Needless to say, that was the last time I interacted with him and quickly found a new doctor.

The antithesis to this was another mutual friend that we had who was always there for both Joe and myself, he did not choose sides, but saw both Joe and myself as worthy human beings. Until I moved to California he continued to interact with both of us equally. Dennis Blair was a model of what is good in people and he represents the perspective and lesson I want to carry forward.

Fifth Lesson: Living in a glass house can have it's advantages

Before coming to Pennsylvania to become the CEO and Dean of Penn State Berks-Lehigh Valley College (the equivalent of being a small college president) my friend and colleague, Dr. Judith Redwine who was Chancellor of State Center Community College District reminded me that being the president or chancellor of a college means that you will live in a glass house. This was something that I already intuitively knew, but I appreciated her reminding me of that fact.

Living in a glass house means that many people in your community know who you are and what you do, even if you have no clue as to who they are. When you walk into the grocery store or the Home Depot, someone will see you and know who you are. People are more likely to accept less than professional attire from a man who lives in a glass house, but there are more raised eyebrows if it is a woman, so I always am tastefully dressed when I leave my home.

What you do and how well you do it, is also known by your community. If you are doing a good job, then there is a greater degree of forgiveness metered out to you. One of the first things I did when I took over at the college was to help our police force on the Berks campus get authorization to carry weapons. Both Fresno and Reading have some things in common and they revolve around crime rates and the potential for undesirable elements to occasionally find their way to the campus. At Berks we are very fortunate to have a top-notch police force, but in spite of the fact that they had "full leather," they had no weapons. The police officers at University Park were the only officers to be authorized to carry a weapon. My colleague who was my counterpart at Penn State Erie, had been trying to get his police authorize without success. Because of my experience in Fresno, I was able to present a perspective, backed by data that showed our officers were vulnerable because they could not defend themselves against those elements that might come into the area. Additionally, our police officers were called in as back-ups on occasions by the local police forces. In relatively short order our officers were certified and authorized. This made them very happy and it was viewed as a very good thing by the surrounding police forces.

Recently I was driving down a country road—literally down as in downhill. My mind was on some event at work and I was not paying attention to my speed. Pretty soon I saw the flashing lights behind me; looking down at the speedometer I knew I was in BIG trouble! The officer came to the window and took my registration and license and walked back to his car. Now my driver's license does not say Dr. Speece, it says Susan Phillips Speece, but when the officer came back the car he said, "Dr. Speece you might want to focus on the road and not on work." He then just asked me to slow down and let me go. I thanked him very much and did slow down. Since I drive that road twice each day, I now put the car on cruise control so I do not let gravity and mind wanderings allow the speed to go beyond an acceptable level.

Did living in a glass house help? What do you think? Rest assured, I do not intend to test the theory any further.

Sixth Lesson: Gasoline vapors travel downhill in humid weather.

I may be a scientist, but there are times when I make major goofs. Recently an acquaintance did a favor and cut some branches for me. I had hoped that they would bundle the branches and put them out for the trash, but they were convinced that I could safely burn them. I live in a wooded, hilly area and was very anxious about doing just that, but finally one day, after several days of rain, I decided to give it a try. Because the wood was wet, I knew I needed to put some accelerant on the pile of brush. The only thing I had was gasoline, so I sloshed a little on the pile three times, then went into the house to get my fireplace matches. These matches were old and just too soggy. After trying unsuccessfully to light about a dozen matches, I went back into the house to get some kitchen matches. I lit one match and threw it into the pile on the hillside. There was a little fizzle so I waited several minutes to be sure nothing was going to catch on. Nothing happened, so I carefully sloshed a little more gasoline onto the pile. Again nothing happened so I boldly put two more sloshes of gasoline on the pile. I carefully closed the gasoline container and placed it a good 20' away from the fire. Careful to not get too close to the pile, I lit yet another match and threw it onto the pile. There was a loud whoosh and pop and the pile exploded into flame. I expected that, what I did not expect was what happened next. Because of the high level of humidity in the air, the accumulated gasoline vapors had stayed on the ground and had rolled down the hill toward and around me. The end result was that there were flames on the surface of the grass all around me and on my lower legs. I back peddled as fast as I could and within seconds the vapors had all burned off. The grass was singed, and so were my ankles.

When the initial explosion took place and I saw the flames on the ground, it was like everything went into slow motion. I looked down and saw that my ankles were aflame, but I was not burning anywhere else. There was a momentary fascination with the burn patterns on the ground and on my body. It did not make sense initially and yet it was also beautiful. Trust me, that was less than one second in duration before I was moving and trying to decide if I needed to "drop and roll." My primary concern was to get the gasoline container further away from the flames.

Someone was watching out for me because I only suffered first and second degree burns on my ankles, which went away in a matter of weeks, but it could have been catastrophic. A few days later I walked back to the spot and could see the wide circle of singed grass with two green footprints where I initially stood. The fact that I am not in a burn unit of a hospital is truly a miracle. Needless to say, I got out my clippers and put the brush out for the trash after that.

20

Serendipity

Serendipity is defined as "an aptitude for making desirable discoveries by accident." I like to think of serendipity as life's surprise parties; those times when you least expect something good, there it is. The question is—are we observant enough to recognize those moments of serendipity, and when we do recognize those moments, what do we do about them?

There have been several examples of serendipity that I have mentioned already; the posting for the California position on the day I decided to see what was happening in California job wise, or the PSU job after talking with a friend about Pennsylvania.

When I moved to Pennsylvania I went through the usual hassle of finding new doctors, electricians, you know the routine. Penn State requires all of its executives to go through an executive physical each year, a practice that I do appreciate. When I was having my administrative assistant schedule my physical at Hershey Medical, she came across a woman physician whom she said was coming highly recommended. That was serendipity!! Dr. Luanne Thorndyke is not just any old physician. First of all, she is not at all old and she is an internist. In the past year she was also named the Associate Dean for Professional Development of the Medical School. More importantly, she has become a dear and treasured friend. We are two women who are passionate about what we do and that we do it well. Finding a kindred spirit has been a boon for both of us. She has come to offer one of our commencement addresses and she did a wonderful job. Recently when I was stressing out over the amount of time I had been spending on the job and finding it difficult to find my life she said, "I am looking in a mirror." We have made a pact to get together from time-to-time just to decompress and refocus.

Likewise I was looking for a jeweler. While in Indiana I had a good friendship with my jewelers. The father was a member of our church and the son was getting more and more involved with running the business. They were and are quality, ethical men whom I trusted. I wanted to find that same kind of friendship with a local jeweler. While I did not get any serious guidance in that department, someone mentioned that there was a new jeweler that had just moved from the south side of town to a shopping village just down the road from my office. Eventually I made my way to Goldsmiths and there met Bob Matt. Bob has become a dear friend who is one of the most gifted artists I have known. He has made several stunning pieces of jewelry for me that always garner praise. Hopefully some of those folks have gone his way as a result. Serendipity—had Bob not moved his store to a location that I had spotted, I might have missed out on a wonderful friendship. Perhaps the friendship was also a bit serendipitous for Bob as well. When he ended a passionate love affair and engagement, I was able to be there for him as he tried to find his footing again. We were able to talk about just about anything and the catharsis was good for both of us.

Another wonderful example of serendipity lately came about in the spring of 2004. I was overworked to the extreme and took a five-day weekend just to recharge my batteries. I spent two days in Ocean City, MD and one day in Williamsburg, VA. In each case, I was just walking through the motions. I could not unwind enough to enjoy the time away. Finally I headed down to the Outer Banks. I had never been there before and my daughter had been singing their praises. On the drive down, I drove through the eastern peninsula of Virginia and across the "bridge-tunnel." On the drive down route 13 I spotted some wildlife sculptures that looked very familiar. As I was speeding down the highway I noticed the foundry for the artist responsible for these sculptures. I made a mental note to stop on the way back if I had time. The pieces were ones I had seen across the country and the work was beautiful and powerful. You too have probably seen this artist's work–a large outdoor sculpture with Canadian Geese rising from the cattails. The Outer Banks were great. The weather was miserable, but I still enjoyed the time down there and will likely go back sometime.

I needed to make the trek back to Pennsylvania, so I was on my way on a sunny Monday morning. I remembered the sculptures, but thought I had missed the studio and had stopped looking. Suddenly there was a huge billboard proclaiming Turner Sculpture Foundry 12 miles on the port side. I had to chuckle at the nautical reference. Sure enough, 12 miles down the road I spotted the foundry. I almost did not stop, but decided I was still on vacation time and I owed it to myself to check it out. I entered the building, which is a mixture of museum and showroom, with several buildings behind that comprise the working studios and foundry. As I walked into the first room there were several old black and white photos of the artist working on a sculpture. I figured they were about 20 years old, given the clothes and hairstyles. I was enjoying a leisurely exploration of the room, when I turned around and realized the artist was in the room. I said hello and told him that I had enjoyed his work around the country. We chatted a while and he asked if I had come across the bridge-tunnel. That is an experience in and of itself! Our conversation was relaxed and easy, but we were interrupted by a young man who came in and said, "Dr. Turner, we are ready to pour." The artist's response was "Yea, I'll be right there." When he turned back to me, he stopped and then asked if I would like to see them pour the moulds. I have always had a fascination with artistic creation so I jumped at the chance. The bronze having been poured, he then took me through his entire processing, introduced me to his partner and middle son and then told me about the book he was writing. It was to be the third in a trilogy about his life. We talked about it for a while and I mentioned that I often did some editing and would be happy to look at it if he would like. Keep in mind that letting someone else look at and even edit your work can be a real leap of faith for any writer. Bill Turner is a delightful and talented storyteller.

Suffice it to say, that the one stop at the foundry has lead to a warm friendship. A delightful, blue crab, bronze graces my hearth, and I am sure there will be more bronzes to come. More importantly, on that spring day I just happened by and life handed me a wonderful surprise.

Bill did trust me with his manuscript and we discussed his book and my edits over breakfast one morning in Seaford, DL. I was going through some minor suggestions, but there were a few questions that I had that were of more substance. We were quietly talking about the book as we sat side-by-side in a wide booth. We had been there for a while discussing the book when the folks in a booth near us got up to leave. The woman came up and admitted that she had been shamelessly eavesdropping. She wanted to know if he was writing a book. That was confirmed and she was soooo thrilled that on that very morning, the morning she and her husband had gone out for breakfast, we would be there discussing a new book. She wanted to know what he did and he modestly stated that he had a little foundry where they made bronze sculptures. I corrected, indicating that his work was known around the world. I thought the poor woman would pass out from hyperventilating. For her, that breakfast was definitely a serendipity moment.

21

Promises Kept

The persistent summer rain accompanied by an occasional rumble of thunder has turned my home into a jewel of a fairyland. The prismatic effect of the raindrops has turned greens into verdant greens, the red of the geranium into vibrant red and the white of the petunia into brilliant white. It is as if Mother Nature has enveloped me in the richest, most lush quilt of colors. The few open windows allow in the rich fragrances of damp earth, a hint of pine, a tickle of jasmine, and a delicious mix of other aromas that are unique to my little slice of heaven here on earth. Even the birds seem filled with joy at the bath they are receiving. It is a wonderful time to just enjoy the gifts of nature and to reflect on the gifts of a lifetime.

As I promised Dr. Thorndyke, I am taking time just for me. I have promised to try and keep, to a minimum, the number of eighty-hour weeks. They are unavoidable and will happen if I want to do my job well, but I can say no a little more often. I actually scheduled in a week and a half off this summer and decided to spend the time at home. My good friend and fellow college president Dr. Richard Kratz, chided me recently for not going away for my vacation, but I knew that I would be recuperating from some minor foot surgery and I really like my home, so that is where I am. It also gives me the opportunity to put the finishing touches on this reflection. When I come home at night I always feel as though I am coming to a retreat. It might not be the cabin in the woods, but with more than a hundred trees on the two acres, it comes pretty close.

The first home that Joe and I purchased was 900 square feet of modular, prefabricated home. It was a great starter home, but as I look around at the home I have now, I realize just how blessed I have been. It is not so much the actual house or its size that I reflect on—that is just "stuff," but it is the collection of memorabilia within the home that represents the journey of my life. There are the photographs I have taken that are worthy of enlarging and framing. The work is good, but the memories of the taking of each are even more important. There is the one photograph that I took while flying in a KC-135 as we were refueling an A-10, now that was a real kick! Or the photo I caught as two young Amish girls with inline skates held fast to the back of the buggy and were being towed down the city street by their family and the family horse. There are some pieces of artwork that I have picked up in my travels around the world and there are several of my own paintings that show a true evolution of style. Early on, I would paint when I did not know how to deal with the pain in my life. I would choose still-lifes—fixed images that I could control and use to try and bring a little beauty into my life. Now my paintings are very abstract and represent a free expression of impressions. There is both movement and joy in my paintings now. I would NEVER claim to be an artist, but last year an artist whose work I greatly admire, paid me an incredible compliment. I wanted to commission him to create a piece that I would put with a collection of Grand Canyon/Southwest photography. He creates his own paper and then sculpts it into beautiful works of art. When Ed Babiarz and his partner Tim Greusel, came to my home to see where I planned to display his art, he said that he would create the piece for me if I would paint a picture for him. Oh my gosh!!! I paint just for me, but to have a real artist want one of my pieces was just such high praise. I think I got the better end of the deal, but to my delight, he is as thrilled with my painting for him as I am with his beautiful creation. Even more gratifying is the fact that Tim and Ed believe in my art so much that they gave me a year's membership in a local artists' guild.

There was a sign I used to have hanging in my office when I taught at Anderson University. It said: "People were made to be loved and things were made to be used. We get into trouble when we reverse the process and love things and use people." When I talk about the "things" in my home it is the memories of people and events that are important to me. I have tried to live my life remembering the importance of the people in my life. Through this reflection I have tried to raise up some of the special people I have known over the years. To be sure, there are many more whom I have not mentioned, but each has contributed a fiber that has been woven into the tapestry of my life. There have been those who would also represent some of the negative experiences in my life and most I have omitted, yet they too have contributed fibers to the tapestry. Without the dark experiences it is difficult to fully appreciate the brilliant colors of the good.

Through those difficult times in my life, I truly believe that it has been my relationship with a loving and fair God that has sustained me. I am not impressed with organized religions, though I have always been a part of one church or another. What impresses me and guides me are the acts of kindness that we see in people. I really believe that, in spite of myself, a force much greater than I has opened doors for me. I believe that that force is available for everyone and when I do a motivational speech, particularly for young people, I encourage them to watch for those opened doors. Sometimes we are so wrapped up in what we want or think should happen that we miss the opportunity opening before us. It is somewhat like the joke that circulates in both Christian and Jewish congregations.

A man was in his home when the storms began and the flooding soon surround his home. In time the water was at his door and some rescue folks were in a little boat telling him to get in and they would take him to safety. The man declined, stating that he was a man of faith and knew that God would not take his life. A few hours later he was on his roof because the waters had risen so far. A large motorboat came along and offered to save him, but again he said he was a man of faith and knew that God would not take his life. Finally a helicopter came by as he was perched on his chimney and offered to save him, but again he declined with the same reason. The next thing the man knew he was standing before God, complaining, asking God why He had not saved him. God's response was, "What the heck did you want, I sent you a small boat, a big motorboat and a helicopter, but you refused."

Sometimes life does not happen the way we envisioned it to be, but when we allow life to happen, it is so much better than our limited imaginations might conceive. As a youth, when I dreamed of what my life would be like, I could not have imagined being a dean at a community college or a CEO of a branch campus of a land grant university. I knew I wanted to have children, but I could never have imagined the incredibly wonderful two adults whom I have had the honor of raising. It is true likewise that I did not imagine the depth of pain I would know when my heart was broken or that love could lift one so high. Yet when one embraces all that life has to offer and you are willing to step into those open doors, the gifts of life are beyond description.

22

Peace Like a River/On the Dock

As a young woman standing on the brink of adulthood, I always thought that marriage was forever. Knowing that I could not keep my marriage whole, along with some longstanding insecurity from my childhood, left me shaken after my divorce. While I never doubted my competence professionally, I had my doubts about my desirability as a woman. I was clearly caught between the old image of the woman as the homemaker and the modern image of the woman as a career minded member of society. Two cultures were on a collision course within me. In addition, the attempted sexual assault as a child, the several sexual harassments that took place both at Purdue and Anderson did not turn me against men, but caused me to doubt my worth as a woman. Thankfully there was one man who came into my life at the very time that I needed it most. He was a professional; a colleague and he understood the challenges of academe. He knew the discipline so we always had something to discuss. Amazingly enough to me, he also found me very desirable. For the first time in my life, I really was able to understand what it was like to be totally valued, loved and appreciated–all of me–the professional me and the personal me. It was a heady feeling and one desperately needed at that point in my life. I will be forever indebted to that wonderful man. Circumstances and distance would work against us and over time we drifted apart. The good news is that we are still good friends and we check up on each other from time-to-time.

Over the years I have been fortunate to meet some wonderful men, but there have only been a few serious relationships. Given my job transitions, meeting men has not been easy. I do not want this to be a Hollywood tell-all book, it profits no one, but the point that I make here is that I choose life and I choose to live it from a positive perspective. There have been broken hearts, but I am still hopeful that love is possible. I do not think we ever get too old to love; certainly the information coming out of nursing homes validates that perspective. Now that my professional life is so satisfying I am hopeful that my personal life can reach the same level.

Early on in my reflections, I mentioned love at first sight. The second time I experienced that and perhaps the truest example of it, took place a few years ago. I had met a man via the Internet (hey, what can I say, I am a techno geek.) He clearly was articulate, a successful president of a Philadelphia area corporation, and one who had had some similar life experiences. We communicated for about two months and then I invited him to come to a concert. He planned to spend two days in Reading and he checked into the Sheraton Hotel. When I went to pick him up at the hotel and he stepped toward my car, I knew I was done looking! The evening together at the concert and the next morning when we got together again for breakfast, just confirmed that I had found the man of my dreams. My love continued to grow through the intervening two years. We never lacked for conversation, we both respected each other tremendously and we both admired what each had accomplished in life. More importantly, I trusted him completely and we really liked the person we were sharing time with. He also knew just the right thing to say. Several months after we had first met, we were slated to have lunch together, sort of a "pre-Christmas" lunch. I was going to be in Philadelphia for a memorial service for one of my faculty members. We had agreed upon a time and location to meet, but the service ran later than I expected. I hate being late, but there was no helping it this time, I was about 30 minutes late. When I got to the restaurant he was delighted to see me, not at all peeved. We greeted each other with kisses and hugs, which left red lipstick on his lips. I reached over to wipe off the lipstick and kidded him that it did not look as good on him as it did me. He had the perfect comeback. "If it is your shade, then it is the right shade." I thought I would melt right then and there.

While I was in love, the irony of life is that he was not ready to move into a serious relationship and so once again, I had a very good and dear friend and a chaste relationship. While the realization that our friendship would never be more than just that was painful, I am richer for having known him. For now I will embrace the life I have and all the possibilities it holds.

As the sun warmed my body and a gentle breeze tickled my senses, Redwing blackbirds, laughing gulls, gold finches, cardinals and more, created an age-old song that lulled me in the idyllic setting of the Virginia dock. As I lay on the dock, enfolded by sights and sounds in this isolated eastern Virginia wilderness, I also thought of how my life has come full circle. There are times when I do feel the press of 'aloneness' but when I put things into perspective, I know that I have been blessed by the experiences of my life. There was a line in a book I read recently, "Good memories are like charms…Each is special. You collect them, one by one, until one day you look back and discover they make a long, colorful bracelet." James Patterson *Suzanne's Diary for Nicholas*. My reflections here have been like looking at one's beautiful life bracelet and remembering each gem with fondness and joy.

Days before my mini-get-away to the cabin in the Virginia woods, I had had a totally delightful experience with a group of young women. One of my faculty members, on an annual basis, organizes a conference for young women who are interested in sciences, mathematics and technology. They come to the college for a day of interactions with faculty and community women who have careers in the sciences, mathematics, and technology. For the past two years I have had the pleasure of serving as the keynote speaker. This year, the questions were more active and I was having fun interacting with these young 13 year-old girls. One young woman asked what in my career had given me the greatest satisfaction– very insightful question coming from one so young. I indicated that after raising two wonderful children, which is number one on my list, I guess it was helping James Ross achieve a degree of autonomy with his new van. It was not being named a Fellow of the American Association for the Advancement of Science in 2001, it was not serving on the Chair's Advisory Council for the development of the *National Science Education Standards*, it was not being named a Berks County Woman of Distinction in 2003, it was not even the thousands of students that I had challenged to be all that they could. It was the act of kindness that others had overlooked that filled me the most. I do not mean to pat myself on my back, that is not it at all. It is just that I know one human being's life is significantly better because I asked others to be all that they could be and they rose to the challenge. My answer surprised the young woman and in fact you could hear a pin drop in the room for several moments. I hope that the young women in that room under-stood the *power of one* in those moments.

The next question came from a smiling young girl who asked if I was always so positive–she caught me off guard, but I had to say that I guess I have always been so, even when life tried to convince me otherwise. I know I can always hear the song of the Redwing Blackbird and there is hope for tomorrow.

Photo number	Description	Photographer
Photo 1 Cover	Redwing Blackbird	Susan Phillips Speece
Photo 2	VA dock	SPS
Photo 3	Redwing Blackbird	SPS
Photo 4	Pat and G. Truman Phillips	taken 1935 photographer unknown
Photo 5	Truman & Susan	taken 1949 phot. unkn.
Photo 6	Susan	taken 1949 phot. unkn.
Photo 7	Ella Phillips	circa 1935 phot. unkn.
Photo 8	Cousins and spouses	SPS
Photo 9	Dave Smith & Susan	circa 1960 phot. unkn.
Photo 10	Joe and Susan	my parents
Photo 11	Ryan & Nicole	circa 1977 phot. unkn.
Photo 12	Pond in our back yard	SPS
Photo 13	Colorado River at Lee's Ferry	SPS
Photo 14	Vasey's Paradise	SPS
Photo 15	Anasazi Granaries	SPS
Photo 16	Nankoweap	SPS
Photo 17	Havasu	SPS
Photo 18	Lava Falls	SPS
Photo 19	Family Room	SPS
Photo 20	Samantha	SPS
Photo 21	Rain soaked deck	SPS
Photo 22	Tulpehocken Creek	SPS
Photo 23	Queen Ann's Lace	SPS
Photo 24	Redwing Blackbird	SPS
Photo 25	Susan Phillips Speece	SPS

0-595-34526-3

Printed in the United States
35208LVS00003B/157-177

9 780595 345267